MIGRANTS AND CITIZENS

Migrants and Citizens

Justice and Responsibility
in the Ethics of Immigration

Tisha M. Rajendra

WILLIAM B. EERDMANS PUBLISHING COMPANY
GRAND RAPIDS, MICHIGAN

Wm. B. Eerdmans Publishing Co.
2140 Oak Industrial Drive N.E., Grand Rapids, Michigan 49505
www.eerdmans.com

Published 2017
Printed in the United States of America

26 25 24 23 22 21 20 19 18 17   1 2 3 4 5 6 7 8 9 10

ISBN 978-0-8028-6882-4

Library of Congress Cataloging-in-Publication Data

Names: Rajendra, Tisha M., 1977– author.
Title: Migrants and citizens : justice and responsibility in the ethics of immigration /
  Tisha M. Rajendra.
Description: Grand Rapids, Michigan : Eerdmans Publishing Co., 2017. |
  Includes bibliographical references and index.
Identifiers: LCCN 2017008126 | ISBN 9780802868824 (pbk. : alk. paper)
Subjects: LCSH: Emigration and immigration—Moral and ethical aspects. |
  Emigration and immigration—Religious aspects—Christianity. |
  Social justice—Religious aspects—Christianity. | Social ethics. | Christian ethics.
Classification: LCC JV6038 .R34 2017 | DDC 241/.622—dc23
  LC record available at https://lccn.loc.gov/2017008126

Contents

Foreword

In the summer of 2013, hundreds of refugees packed onto a rickety boat on the shores of the Libyan coast and ventured forth into the open sea. They were fleeing social unrest, political persecution, and human rights abuses and hoped to find a safe place to land, anywhere that would receive them. While en route their vessel capsized, and most of them drowned in the middle of the Mediterranean. A few survived the shipwreck by clinging to the fishing nets of a nearby Tunisian boat, and when they saw fishermen in the distance, they pleaded desperately to be saved. When the fishermen saw them holding on to their lines, however, they cut them loose and sent them to die in the ocean depths.

One of those who heard about this story was the newly elected Pope Francis. He was so moved by their plight that he wanted to make "a gesture of closeness" with these refugees and to challenge the conscience of the world, "lest this tragedy be repeated." Eight days later he made his first pastoral visit outside of the Vatican to the small and isolated Italian island of Lampedusa, located in the middle of the waters between Africa and Europe. More than 5,000 died in these waters in 2016,[1] adding to the more than 40,000 migrants who have died on their journeys since the year 2000.[2]

Shortly after arriving, Pope Francis celebrated the Eucharist near the island harbor, next to a "boat graveyard," where the remains of migrant ships pile up. In preparation for the mass, a local carpenter crafted the

---

1. For the latest statistics on migrant deaths, see the Missing Migrants Webpage of the International Organization of Migration, https://missingmigrants.iom.int.

2. International Organization for Migration, "Fatal Journeys: Tracking Lives Lost During Migration" (2014): 15.

altar from a migrant boat's hull, the lectern from ships' rudders, and the chalice from driftwood of downed vessels.[3] Through words, gestures, and symbols Pope Francis reminded us of the integral relationship between the bodies of these refugees and the body of Christ and our call to solidarity with the least and the last among us. Amidst a world growing increasingly indifferent to their plight, he sought to weave a renewed narrative in society about who God is, who we are, and who we are called to be to each other.

In dramatic contrast to this narrative, Donald Trump has sought to weave a different one, especially about migrants, refugees, and our response to them. Shortly after launching his campaign he said, "When Mexico sends its people, they're not sending their best. . . . They're not sending you. They're sending people that have lots of problems, and they're bringing those problems with us. They're bringing drugs. They're bringing crime. They're rapists. And some, I assume, are good people."[4] Even when presented with a mountain of empirical data and research to the contrary, Trump and his supporters continued to advance this narrative. Not only was it politically expedient, but it also spoke to the fears and insecurities of many people, who wanted some remedy to social upheaval, economic uncertainty, and a weakening sense of national identity. After he was elected, Trump sought to translate that narrative into public policy by initiating a series of executive orders aimed at excluding refugees and directed toward building a "beautiful wall" that would separate "us" from "them."

The narrative of Pope Francis and the narrative of Donald Trump highlight two different ways of interpreting and responding to the complex challenges posed by global migration. In between these two narratives, there is much conflict, controversy, and confusion, which points to the need not only for more information but for a new imagination about how to think about it. This profound and thoughtful work by Tisha Rajendra seeks to take on this challenge, and she goes to the heart of the issue when she asks probing questions about the quality of our relationships. In particular she challenges us to consider the question, who is responsible for protecting migrants? This question is not easy to resolve, and

3. For more on this topic, see Daniel G. Groody, "Cup of Suffering, Chalice of Salvation," *Theological Studies* (forthcoming 2017).

4. https://www.washingtonpost.com/news/fact-checker/wp/2015/07/08/donald -trumps-false-comments-connecting-mexican-immigrants-and-crime/?utm_term=. 6f9488720fd4.

the present context that divides the narrative into traditional dualisms like citizen/alien, legal/illegal, and native/foreigner have broken down. Not only do these categories not work but they also create waves of injustice that force countless individuals into the shadows of society and make them vulnerable to being exploited on the merciless sea of human indifference.

As she helps us untangle the complex challenges posed by migration, Rajendra not only gives us a way of understanding the conceptual terrain of migration but also addresses the cognitive, spiritual, and ethical undercurrent that shapes our moral imagination. At the heart of her reflection is the search for a more life-giving narrative that moves us from social fragmentation to right relationships. Because narratives within us continually govern our thoughts, our actions, and our policies, she helps us examine new ways of thinking about immigrants that move us beyond the politics of "otherness" and toward a vision of "oneness."

Rajendra's work, then, is not just another book on immigration. It is fundamentally a book about relationships and ethical foundations needed for building a more just and humane society. The US Bishops have repeatedly affirmed that the single most important criterion of the health of a society is how it treats its most vulnerable members and how it responds to the needs of the poor through its public policies.[5]

As a work in Christian ethics, this book is guided by the conviction that each human life is profoundly interconnected with others in a series of overlapping relationships. Rajendra reminds us that we do not live as isolated islands but are embedded into a series of interconnected relationships with God, others, and the natural world. She highlights the need for humanizing activity that leads to right relationships with one's self, the community, its social structures, and finally the environment itself. These relationships are central to the process of human flourishing and global transformation.

Reframing the topic of migration in light of these relationships, Rajendra has helped us see that migration is not the central problem we face today but the symptom of deeper problems that force people to leave their homelands and seek dignity and opportunities in a new land. The issues presented in the pages that follow are significant for many reasons, and they help us remember that if we choose to be ruled by the politics of fear rather than a

---

5. United States Conference of Catholic Bishops, Economic Justice for All, no. 8, available at http://www.usccb.org/upload/economic_justice_for_all.pdf.

social ecology of interconnected relationships, then what is at stake is not just the deportation of immigrants but the deportation of our hearts and souls as well.[6]

DANIEL G. GROODY, CSC
University of Notre Dame

---

6. For more on these topics, see Bill Ong Hing, *Deporting Our Souls: Values, Morality, and Immigration Policy* (Cambridge: Cambridge University Press, 2006), and Susanna Snyder, *Asylum-Seeking, Migration and Church* (Burlington, VT: Ashgate, 2012).

Acknowledgments

I wrote this book with the support, in part, of a Summer Research Stipend and a Junior Faculty Research Leave, both from Loyola University of Chicago.

I am extraordinarily grateful to be a part of a vibrant community of theologians and ethicists. Sandra Sullivan Dunbar, Devorah Schoenfeld, Hille Haker, and Maria McDowell have all played a part in my scholarly and intellectual formation. Sandy, Devorah, and Maria all read drafts of various chapters of this book, and it is infinitely better due to their careful reading and insightful critiques. The seeds of the book were developed in my PhD dissertation, which was directed by David Hollenbach. Jeffrey Campbell, my research assistant, helped me with the bibliography. My two editors-in-chief at Eerdmans Publishing Company, Jon Pott and James Ernest, pressed me toward greater clarity and discipline in writing and challenged me to write a book that others would actually want to read. I thank them for their patience during what turned out to be a long process.

A great deal of upheaval, unrelated to the writing process, accompanied the writing of this book. The friendship and assistance of so many made it possible for me to continue writing through the turmoil. In particular, I wish to thank Nicholas E. Morrell and his team at Morgan Lewis, Neela Rajendra, Denise Nepveux, Claire Purkis, M. T. Dávila, Ramón Luzárraga, Aana Vigen, Catherine Wolf, and Susan Ross, the chair of the Department of Theology at Loyola.

My husband, co-parent, and life partner, Dana Houle, has unfailingly believed that I had something worth saying. The uneven distribution of childcare responsibilities in our household enabled me to say it. Our children, Julian and Miriam, born while I was writing this book, make me laugh every single day. Finally, I wish to thank my parents, Clement and Subi Rajendra, my first teachers of justice and responsibility.

Introduction

"People are on the move"—so goes a popular expression, and any cursory examination of migration in the twenty-first century shows that this is so. More than 3 percent of the world's population—over 215 million people—live outside the country in which they are citizens. While migration to and from poor countries is on the rise, seven of the top ten destination countries for migrants are Western liberal democracies.[1] In these countries, immigration has become a hot-button political issue. The free migration between European Union countries was cited as a key reason why many British citizens voted to leave the EU in July 2016. In the United States, presidential candidate Donald Trump successfully campaigned on promises to seal the border between Mexico and the United States, and to deport millions of undocumented migrants. As I write this, many in France fear the growing power of the far-right-wing *Front National*, which advocates restricting immigration and favoring French citizens over immigrants in the labor and housing markets.

As xenophobic rhetoric increases throughout the United States and Europe, complex questions of immigration policy are reduced to questions of how to keep migrants out. In the United States, Trump's pledge to build a wall along the southern US border with Mexico was front and center in his appeal to a certain segment of the American voting public. In Austria, a fence on the Hungarian border is there to keep migrants from entering. The Spanish enclaves of Ceuta and Melilla are demarcated from the rest of the continent of Africa by chainlink fences. In France, Marine Le Pen argues for

1. The top ten countries of destination are the United States, Russia, Germany, Saudi Arabia, Canada, the United Kingdom, Spain, France, Australia, and India. Available at: http://peoplemov.in (accessed December 5, 2016).

revoking EU agreements to free cross-border movement and for reinstating border checks.

Yet the issue of border security, which assumes that noncitizens have no right to be in the territory, often obscures a whole host of human-rights issues surrounding migration. The first human-rights issue is that these attempts to secure borders result in the deaths of migrants. No matter how high the walls, no matter how dangerous the sea or desert, migrants remain undeterred in their quests to reach their countries of destination. Every year, hundreds of migrants perish in the Sonoran desert of Mexico in their attempts to find homes in the United States. In 2015 alone, 2,600 migrants drowned in the Mediterranean Sea en route to Europe. The deaths of these migrants are casualties of the right of the states to protect their borders.

A second set of ethical issues has to do with the fact that, though migrants enter countries in spite of border security and immigration policies designed to keep them out, they form a vital part of the economies in many Western democracies. In Western Europe, increased labor migration has even been presented as part of a solution to the problem of rapidly aging populations.[2] The obvious disconnect between border-security policies that use harsh measures to keep migrants out and economies that depend on the contributions of migrants has led to what former US President Barack Obama has called a "shadow society" of undocumented migrants.[3] Migrants are left out of many of the social-safety-net protections of the countries in which they reside. If they are undocumented, they are extraordinarily vulnerable to abuses in the labor and housing markets. They often cannot claim protections to which they are entitled under the law, because doing so would risk deportation. In fact, even legal migrants remain in their host countries by whim rather than by right, and governments can and do deport legal migrants for even minor infractions.

A third set of ethical issues has to do with the cultural integration of migrants.[4] Do migrants have the right to speak their own language? To pass on their own cultural traditions? What if the cultural or religious values of migrants come into conflict with the culture or religion of the majority of citizens?

2. Rainer Münz, "Demography and Migration: An Outlook for the 21st Century," *Migration Policy Institute Policy Brief* 4 (2013).

3. Paul Lewis, "Barack Obama: 'We Are and Always Will Be a Nation of Immigrants,'" *The Guardian*, November 21, 2014, http://www.theguardian.com/us-news/2014/nov/20/obama-plan-shield-five-million-undocumented-migrants-deportation-speech.

4. I avoid the loaded term "assimilation" here.

In much of Europe and the United States, the political debate and rhetoric surrounding immigration often conflates these three different issues. Broadly speaking, participants are usually exclusionists or inclusionists. The exclusionists argue that migrants burden the social welfare state and pose an economic threat to citizens by taking their jobs. This argument undergirds the French *Front National*'s proposals to limit social welfare provisions for immigrants and to favor French citizens in the labor market. American exclusionists often argue that migration poses a security threat to citizens by way of terrorism, drug trafficking, and gang violence. For example, Donald Trump frequently stoked fears of terrorism by suggesting that Syrian refugees were linked to ISIS. Exclusionists also often argue that the cultural and religious values of migrants are inherently incompatible with the values of citizens. Hence, migrants threaten to replace the cultural and religious traditions of citizens with their own. In the face of such threats, exclusionists often propose tightening border security and deporting undocumented migrants.

On the other side, inclusionists argue that, in the face of the tremendous need and suffering of migrants, governments have a humanitarian obligation to admit migrants. Some radical inclusionists argue that liberal democracies do not, in fact, have a right to close their borders at all. Migrants who are already in the territory deserve to share in the benefits of the society to which they have contributed. Undocumented migrants deserve mercy; deporting them would be inhumane. Inclusionists also often note that the United States and many countries in Western Europe are already multicultural, and that there is no reason to suppose that further heterogeneity poses a threat to the cultural heritages of these countries.

In the United States, exclusionist and inclusionist positions map onto to two different narratives about migrants. The exclusionist narrative is that migrants are at best opportunists, and at worst criminals, who take advantage of the wealth and generosity of US citizens. The inclusionist narrative can take two forms: the first is that migrants are vulnerable and poor outsiders fleeing desperate poverty; the second is that migrants have made significant contributions to US society. At times, these narratives overlap as American political discourse attempts to delineate the "good" migrants (the ones fleeing poverty and seeking opportunity) from the "bad" migrants (the drug traffickers and other criminals). Both narratives about migrants intersect with the narratives many US citizens tell themselves about their own origins and identities: that they and their fellow citizens are hard-working, generous, and law-abiding. These qualities are then used either, on the one side, to contrast citizens with migrants, or, on the other side, to argue that migrants are not so different from citizens.

But both of these narratives are false. In this book I argue that justice for migrants depends on asking whether such narratives are true to reality. Where such inquiries reveal inaccuracies, we must replace them with narratives that more accurately capture the relationship between citizens and migrants.

This project enters broader discussions about migration, borders, and citizens in the fields of philosophy and theology. Philosophical and theological treatments of migration rarely fit neatly into the exclusionist-inclusionist division. Philosophical ethics of migration can be broadly grouped into cosmopolitan and communitarian treatments of migration. Cosmopolitans argue that the universal claims of human rights override the right of nation-states to exclude migrants. Joseph Carens, for example, argues that the liberal principles of equality and freedom require liberal democracies to have open borders.[5] On the other hand, communitarians argue that the right of a political community to choose its own members is at the center of what it means to be a self-determining community. Whether they are cosmopolitans or communitarians or something in between, philosophers handle the ethics of migration with considerably more attention to moral complexity and less to extreme rhetoric than politicians often do. The cosmopolitan Carens, for example, admits that nation-states can reasonably reject migrants who pose a security threat.[6] Communitarian Michael Walzer spends a considerable amount of time discussing cases in which the right of the nation-state to choose its own members would be limited by obligations that the nation-state might have toward guest workers or refugees.[7]

Theological treatments of migration pay attention to questions that are different from those of most philosophical ethics of migration. While much in the philosophical ethics of migration examines the question of whether—and under what circumstances—migrants must be admitted into political communities and granted citizenship, many theologies of migration highlight the perspective of the migrants themselves: their hopes, joys, sufferings, resilience, and anxieties for the well-being of themselves and their

5. Joseph H. Carens, *The Ethics of Immigration* (New York: Oxford University Press, 2013).
6. Carens, *Ethics of Immigration*, 30–32.
7. Michael Walzer, *Spheres of Justice: A Defense of Pluralism and Equality* (New York: Basic Books, 1983), chap. 2.

families.[8] Theologians such as Gemma Cruz[9] and Daniel Groody[10] seek to understand Christian theology through a hermeneutic of migration. They argue that the experiences of migrants have been overlooked as a locus of theological reflection and that these experiences reveal an authentic Christian theology.

This insight reflects the contributions of Latin American liberation theology and other contextual theologies that look to the experiences of those on the margins of society as the normative perspectives from which to do theology. Many Christian theologians and ethicists draw explicitly on Latin American liberation theology's category of structural sin to understand migration. Gioacchino Campese,[11] Miguel de la Torre,[12] Kristin Heyer,[13] and Ilsup Ahn[14] have all argued that the political, social, and economic structures that drive migration are unjust. These ethicists, however, turn from examining the theological reflections concerning the experiences of migrants to arguing that the unjust structures that drive migration demand particular ethical responses from Christians in the United States. Many Christian ethicists apply the concepts and insights of Catholic social thought to the phenomenon of migration, drawing on concepts such as human dignity and the global common good, or on church documents that specifically address migration.[15]

8. See, e.g., Kristin E. Heyer, *Kinship across Borders: A Christian Ethic of Immigration* (Washington, DC: Georgetown University Press, 2012). See also Daniel G. Groody, "Fruit of the Vine and Work of Human Hands: Immigration and the Eucharist," in *A Promised Land, a Perilous Journey: Theological Perspectives on Migration*, ed. Daniel G. Groody and Gioacchino Campese (Notre Dame, IN: University of Notre Dame Press, 2008); Gemma Tulud Cruz, *Toward a Theology of Migration: Social Justice and Religious Experience* (New York: Palgrave Macmillan, 2014).

9. Gemma Tulud Cruz, *An Intercultural Theology of Migration: Pilgrims in the Wilderness* (Boston: Brill, 2010); see also Gemma Tulud Cruz, *Toward a Theology of Migration*.

10. Groody, "Fruit of the Vine and Work of Human Hands," in Groody and Campese, *A Promised Land*; see also Daniel G. Groody, *Border of Death, Valley of Life: An Immigrant Journey of Heart and Spirit* (Lanham, MD: Rowman and Littlefield, 2002).

11. Gioacchino Campese, "Beyond Ethnic and National Imagination," in *Religion and Social Justice for Immigrants*, ed. Pierrette Hondagneu-Sotelo (New Brunswick, NJ: Rutgers University Press, 2007). Gioacchino Campese, "¿cuantos Más?: The Crucified Peoples at the U.S.-Mexico Border," in Groody and Campese, *A Promised Land*.

12. Miguel A. de la Torre, *Trails of Hope and Terror: Testimonies on Immigration* (Maryknoll, NY: Orbis, 2009).

13. Heyer, *Kinship across Borders*.

14. Ilsup Ahn, *Religious Ethics and Migration: Doing Justice to Undocumented Workers* (New York: Routledge, 2014).

15. Donald Kerwin and Jill Marie Gerschutz, eds., *And You Welcomed Me: Migration and Catholic Social Teaching* (Lanham, MD: Lexington Books, 2009).

In this book I address questions of political philosophy using specific insights from Christian ethics: What responsibilities do citizens have toward migrants and potential migrants? What is the basis of such responsibilities? While many philosophical theories of justice assign specific political and economic rights to members and nonmembers of a society, the question of who has the responsibility to protect the rights of whom has received far less attention.[16] With relationships between citizens and noncitizens, between the near stranger and the far stranger, becoming increasingly more complex, questions of how to justly assign responsibilities for protecting the rights of migrants have become particularly vexing. The question of who has the responsibility to protect the rights of migrants and potential migrants is a part of these larger questions of global justice. I submit that both cosmopolitan and communitarian theories of justice fall short in responding to these complex questions. Instead, I propose a new definition of justice that can respond to the relationships between citizens and migrants: justice as responsibility to relationships.

In order to arrive at this new definition of justice, I look to Gioacchino Campese's counsel that theologians and ethicists must "get to know the reality of migration as it is, in its complex and multifaceted totality."[17] While theologians and ethicists have listened to the voices and experiences of migrants, they have not as thoroughly and systematically paid attention to the phenomenon of migration itself: What drives migration? What leads migrants to relocate to one country rather than another? While many theologies and ethics of migration assume that migration is driven by poverty and economic inequality alone, migration theorists suggest that migration is caused by specific kinds of preexisting relationships between countries of emigration and countries of immigration, relationships that are often based on what Christian ethicists call "social," or "structural," sin.[18] People are indeed on the move, but they move in specific and bounded ways that are a direct consequence of the relationships between migrants and citizens and the relationships among the migrants themselves.

The setting of ethical questions about migration must, therefore, be these complex relationships that emerge from historical and economic re-

16. See, e.g., John Rawls, *A Theory of Justice* (Cambridge, MA: Belknap Press, Harvard University Press, 1971); Walzer, *Spheres of Justice*; Martha C. Nussbaum, *Creating Capabilities: The Human Development Approach* (Cambridge, MA: Belknap Press, Harvard University Press, 2011).

17. Campese, "Beyond Ethnic and National Imagination," 180.

18. Tisha M. Rajendra, "Justice, Not Benevolence: Catholic Social Thought, Migration Theory, and the Rights of Migrants," *Political Theology* 15, no. 3 (2014): 290–306.

alities. In contrast to many theories of justice that begin from a presumption of an ideal world in which rational actors choose the principles of justice under which they want to live, justice as responsibility to relationships begins from the messy relationships in which migrants and citizens find themselves. There is no neat formula for determining what responsibilities follow from what kinds of relationships. Instead, responsibilities are allocated through social narratives that run beneath the surface of our ideas about justice for migrants. For example, the narrative that US citizens are hard-working, law-abiding types while migrants are criminals looking to free-load off a social safety net leads directly to an exclusionist account of responsibilities in which US citizens have few, if any, responsibilities to outsiders. Similarly, the inclusionist narrative, in which US citizens are generous and compassionate people and migrants are poor and vulnerable strangers, leads to an inclusionist account of responsibilities in which US citizens have preferential responsibilities to migrants.

One of the aims of justice as responsibility to relationships, then, is to examine these hidden narratives. Just accounts of responsibility require narratives that are faithful to reality, both requiring fidelity to historical and social-scientific particularities and paying attention to the voices of those who are often ignored. But this attention to specificity and historicity means that a universal narrative that distributes all responsibilities is not possible.

In this book, therefore, I do not attempt to examine all migration flows to all countries. The majority of my case studies come from just three countries: the United States, Germany, and the United Kingdom. I focus on three kinds of migrations to these countries: colonial, guest-worker, and foreign-investment-driven migrations. Although these case studies omit more groups of migrants than they include, focusing on just a few specific examples yields richer and more complex narratives about the relationships between migrants and citizens in these countries.

In addition, I address economic migration, setting aside the current and pressing issue of political refugees. Although many in the fields of theological and philosophical ethics have argued that economic migrants fleeing poverty are morally equivalent to political refugees fleeing state violence, I am in favor of preserving the distinction. While there is some overlap, these two kinds of migration work differently. Migration-systems theory, which I present in chapter 2, was developed to describe economic migration. Nevertheless, there are similarities between economic migrants and political refugees. Like economic migrants, political refugees are caught in a no man's land where it is not clear who has the responsibility to protect their human rights. Further, like economic migrants, political refugees often move along paths influenced by their relationships with other refugees and, in some cases, with citizens in the host countries. Thus, justice as responsibility to relationships can be used to determine the responsibilities of citizens to political refugees as well.

Though modeled on insights that emerge from an account of justice rooted in biblical texts, an examination of the role that responsibilities and relationships play in theories of justice has relevance outside the field of Christian ethics. Justice as responsibility to relationships makes a contribution to ongoing and vexing philosophical discussions of how to distribute social benefits and burdens among the citizens of the world. Beyond the ethics of migration, the framework of justice as responsibility to relationships can help theologians and philosophers think about the ethical issues surrounding economic globalization, international relations, and any relationships that cross national borders. This framework also has potential to guide reflection on the moral questions surrounding complicity in social sin, especially social sins that have roots in the past.

Though this is a work of Christian ethics, informed by my own training in theology, the assessment of the relationship between migrants and citizens has relevance beyond Christian churches. In order to make better assessments of their responsibilities to migrants, citizens must examine the narratives about migration that they carry with them. Regardless of biblical origins, justice as responsibility to relationships can provide a model for uncovering false narratives and replacing them with ones that are more faithful to the reality of the relationships between citizens and migrants.

Outline of Chapters

Many Christian ethicists have attempted to address the question of responsibilities to migrants by drawing on two foundational principles that have become central to Christian social ethics: universal human rights and the preferential option for the poor. I argue in chapter 1 that although these principles work quite well for issues of poverty and justice in the domestic sphere, human rights and the option for the poor are by themselves inadequate to address issues of transnational justice such as migration. Human-rights discourse has focused on the question of who has rights, rather than the question of who has the duty of protecting the rights of whom. The preferential option for the poor fails to provide guidance for sorting through competing responsibilities. Instead, I propose that both human rights and the option for the poor must operate within a theory of justice that proposes not only norms for distributing social goods, but norms for allocating responsibilities. However, in order to allocate responsibilities for migrants justly, we need a more accurate account of how migration works.

In chapter 2, I survey different migration theories in order to show that the most typical way of describing migration as the result of poverty and inequality in sending countries is, in fact, only one way to account for the phenomenon of migration, termed "neoclassical migration theory." Migration theorists have moved away from this account of migration to others that draw to a greater degree on the social networks of migrants and the global social and economic structures that influence migration. While neoclassical migration theory depends too heavily on an account of the person as an autonomous rational agent, theories of migration that emphasize social structures do so to the neglect of the agency of migrants. Chapter 2 presents migration-systems theory as a social-scientific account of migration that places the individual decisions of migrants in the context of the larger social structures that drive migration. Migration-systems theory presents migration as the result of preexisting relationships between migrants and citizens.

If false narratives lead to inadequate ethics, chapter 3 presents a retelling of the narratives of the relationships between migrants and citizens. Better narratives require an examination of the past, present, and future possibilities of a relationship. Most of this chapter examines the relationships between specific groups of citizens and migrants and investigates how these past relationships impact present-day relationships between migrants and citizens.

I examine philosophical theories of global justice in chapter 4, arguing that behind every theory of justice lurks an account of our responsibilities to one another. John Rawls, Martha Nussbaum, and Onora O'Neill have their theories of global justice that arise from their differing philosophical perspectives—*contractarian*, *capabilities*, and *deontological*. Yet each one fails to respond to the particular relationships that drive migration. An accurate account of responsibilities must be rooted in an accurate account of relationships.

In chapter 5, I propose that since migration is rooted in relationships, an account of justice that is itself relational helps to answer the central question of the book. To that end, I turn in this chapter to the legal material of the Pentateuch, particularly the legal norms for the protection of the resident alien in ancient Israel. I mean to show that the responsibilities that ancient Israel had to the resident aliens in their midst were rooted in a conception of justice as right relationship—with God, with the resident aliens, and with one another.

Chapter 6 takes the biblical perspective on justice as right relationship and develops it into a concept of justice as responsibility to relationships, drawing on theological and philosophical ethics of responsibility. Justice as responsibility to relationships emphasizes the uncertain but necessary task of discerning our responsibilities to others. This task is based on a careful evaluation of the relationships between citizens and particular groups of migrants. In other words, a just response to the problems of international migration requires evaluating the relationships between citizens and particular populations of migrants. This is impossible without the virtue of solidarity, which is a corollary to justice: the deliberate cultivation of right relationships with others in the context of a historical and particular relationship of exploitation.

CHAPTER 1

The Inadequacy of Human Rights and the Preferential Option for the Poor

Mario Alapizco Castro was stranded in Altar, a Sonoran town sixty miles south of the U.S.-Mexico border. He had worked and saved for seven years to pay a "coyote" $8,000 to smuggle him from his hometown of Guatemala City to the United States. Just four months after he had settled into a new job in California, a job that allowed him to send money home and to save for the surgery he needed to repair his congenital heart defect, he was apprehended by US Immigration and Customs Enforcement and deported to Altar. Castro could not make the journey into the United States again because of his illness; it would not allow him to survive the rigors of the journey a second time. With no money to pay for transport back to Guatemala City, he was neither here nor there.

Mario Castro was only one of the hundreds of migrants staying in shelters along the US-Mexico border that journalist Margaret Regan encountered in her research for her book *The Death of Josseline* (2010).[1] Like Castro, some of these migrants had been deported from the United States and were stranded on the wrong side of the border; others were preparing themselves for the long and dangerous trek across the Arizona desert. The story of Mario Castro and others who risk their lives to provide a better life for themselves and their children is repeated all over the world. Some migrants risk drowning in the Mediterranean Sea en route to Continental Europe from Africa; others journey across the Sahara Desert in hopes of scaling the fences of the Spanish enclaves of Ceuta and Melilla. The dangers of the journey and the enormous vulnerabilities these migrants experience if and when they arrive at their destination raise crucial issues for any Christian ethics of migration.

1. Margaret Regan, *The Death of Josseline: Immigration Stories from the Arizona-Mexico Borderlands* (Boston: Beacon, 2010).

Mario Castro and many other migrants stranded at the US-Mexico border are citizens of neither the United States nor Mexico. Similarly, African migrants apprehended at the borders of Ceuta and Melilla are usually citizens of neither Morocco nor Spain. The division of the world into a system of territorially sovereign states makes some people citizens and others migrants. Had Mario Castro been a citizen of the United States, he would not have been deported. He might have qualified for Medicaid and Social Security and would have his heart surgery and recovery taken care of. Had he been a citizen, he might have been able to sponsor his wife and children on a family reunification visa. However, Mario Castro was not a citizen of the United States. The US government did not owe him anything at all; in fact, it deported him at the first opportunity. The nation-state system protects citizens and enables them to provide essential goods for one another, but it does not grant noncitizens the same protections.

Castro was not a citizen of the United States, but he was a citizen of another country—Guatemala. While Regan does not explain why Castro decided to make the dangerous and expensive journey north, we can surmise that it had something to do with his desire to provide for his wife and three children back in Guatemala City, and perhaps to secure medical treatment for himself. Castro's lack of access in the country of his birth to goods that many would count as basic human rights—medical care and a living wage that would enable him to support his family—surely spurred his decision to make the dangerous journey to the United States.

Mario Castro's predicament raises critical questions about human rights, migration, and responsibilities. Stranded between two countries, Castro is unable to claim basic protection of his rights in either the United States or Mexico. Yet, if human rights are indeed universal, then surely Castro's claim on the citizens of both the United States and Mexico should be broader than the right to humane treatment during deportation. But while documents like the UN Convention on the Rights of Migrants are quite insistent that migrants are endowed with rights by virtue of their very humanity, few UN statements or academic books discuss who has the duty to protect the rights of migrants and why. This is the case even in Christian ethics, even though the idea that human rights are linked to duties is one with a long history in the field. Yet most Christian ethics of migration do not directly address the question of who has responsibility for protecting the rights of migrants and on what basis these responsibilities are allocated. This is the central question that any ethics of migration must answer: What responsibilities do citizens have to noncitizens?

The importance of this question is not limited to the ethics of migration. What responsibilities do the residents of wealthy, developed nations have to those who live in desperate poverty around the world? Are these responsibilities the same as our responsibilities to the homeless person we pass on the way to work? Are these responsibilities the same as the responsibilities of citizens to the undocumented migrants already in their midst?

Many Christian ethicists have addressed these questions by drawing on two foundational principles that have become central to Christian social ethics: universal human rights and the preferential option for the poor. This chapter argues that, though these principles work quite well for issues of poverty and justice in the domestic sphere, they are by themselves inadequate to address issues of transnational justice such as migration. Human rights and the option for the poor—in focusing on the rights of migrants and the claims they have by virtue of their poverty and vulnerability—do so without allocating responsibility for who must protect their rights and respond to their claims.

Christian Ethics and the Problem with Human Rights

Christian migration ethics has generally answered the question of responsibilities to noncitizens by affirming the full humanity and dignity of migrants: migrants are humans made in the image of God.[2] Regardless of their citizenship, their legal status, or their ethnicity, every person is "a child of God" who "bears the image of Christ."[3] Migrants, created in the image of God, have an inherent dignity that must be protected by human-rights laws. These theological claims are common to both Catholic[4] and

2. Pope John Paul II, "Undocumented Migrants" (message of Pope John Paul II for World Migration Day, 1996; Vatican, July 25, 1995), http://w2.vatican.va/content/john-paul-ii/en/messages/migration/documents/hf_jp-ii_mes_25071995_undocumented_migrants.html.

3. Pope Francis, "Migrants and Refugees: Towards a Better World" (message of His Holiness Pope Francis for the World Day of Migrants and Refugees [2014], Vatican, August 5, 2013), http://w2.vatican.va/content/francesco/en/messages/migration/documents/papa-francesco_20130805_world-migrants-day.html.

4. United States Conference of Catholic Bishops and Conferencia del Episcopado Mexicano, "Strangers No Longer: Together on the Journey of Hope," January 22, 2003, http://www.usccb.org/issues-and-action/human-life-and-dignity/immigration/strangers-no-longer-together-on-the-journey-of-hope.cfm. See also Donald Kerwin, "The Natural Rights of Migrants and Newcomers: A Challenge to U.S. Law and Policy," in Groody and Campese, *A Promised Land.*

Protestant[5] ethics of migration, and to both academic and pastoral Christian ethics.

The commitment to the human rights of migrants means that, though they are not citizens, migrants can make moral claims against the state and its citizens. These claims include a whole host of positive rights, such as the right to employment, a living wage, food and water,[6] in addition to negative rights such as freedoms from interference with rights of association, speech, and self-determination.[7] When these rights are in danger at home, a person has the right to migrate. In other words, when migration becomes a matter of survival for people and their families, the right to leave the country of one's birth and enter another becomes a human right. In the Catholic tradition, because rights are always linked to duties, this right to migrate is linked to the duty of nation-states to welcome migrants.[8] The Christian ethics of migration are refreshingly bold in this insistence on the human rights of migration. In contrast to public-policy discussions about migrants, which rarely begin with the radical notion that migrants are people,[9] Christian ethics of migration affirm both the person's right of immigration and the state's duty to welcome needy migrants, going far beyond the rights accorded to migrants in international law.[10]

This emphasis on human rights leads to a moral cosmopolitanism in which Christian commitment to our own countries and our fellow citizens cannot outweigh our commitment to the worldwide community that ex-

5. House of Bishops of the Episcopal Church, "The Nation and the Common Good: Reflections on Immigration Reform" (The Episcopal Church, September 21, 2010), http://archive.episcopalchurch.org/documents/HOB_theological_resource_on_immigration.pdf.

6. Pope John XXIII, *Pacem in terris*, in *Catholic Social Thought: The Documentary Heritage*, ed. David J. O'Brien and Thomas A. Shannon (Maryknoll, NY: Orbis, 1992), paras. 11–27.

7. Pope John XXIII, *Pacem in terris*, paras. 15, 23.

8. The duty applies only if the nation-state is able to welcome migrants without a risk to public well-being within its own borders. See Drew Christiansen, "Movement, Asylum, Borders: Christian Perspectives," *International Migration Review* (Spring 1996): 7–17; see also Pope Pius XII, *Exsul Familia Nazarethana*, Papal Encyclicals Online, August 1, 1952, http://www.papalencyclicals.net/Pius12/p12exsul.htm. See also United States Conference of Catholic Bishops and Conferencia del Episcopado Mexicano, "Strangers No Longer: Together on the Journey of Hope."

9. Andrew Yuengert and Gloria L. Zúñiga, *Inhabiting the Land: The Case for the Right to Migrate* (Grand Rapids: Acton Institute, 2003).

10. Donald Kerwin, "Rights, the Common Good, and Sovereignty," in Kerwin and Gerschutz, *And You Welcomed Me*, 98–99. The UN Declaration of Human Rights gives people the right to leave their countries but not the right to enter another country.

tends beyond the borders of our own countries.[11] In this reasoning, the good of the nation-state cannot be secured at the expense of the human rights of migrants. For migration ethics and policy, this cosmopolitanism means that the right of the nation-state to control migration is limited by the obligations of the entire political community to the global common good. States should not refuse entry to migrants solely on the basis of national interest.

Basing a Christian ethics of migration on universal human rights has much to recommend it. In contrast to public discourse that dehumanizes migrants, Christian ethics insists on that radical principle that migrants are people. Instead of focusing on how migrants might have broken the law by crossing borders, human-rights discourse draws attention to the ways that migrants are already the victims of injustice. Instead of coupling human rights to citizenship in one nation-state, Christian ethics insists that migrants have rights by virtue of their very humanity.[12] Instead of reducing migrants to what Pope Francis has termed "pawns on the chessboard of humanity," Christian ethics opens us up to the possibility that citizens have responsibilities and obligations to migrants.[13]

Despite the promise of this approach, the asymmetrical emphasis on the human rights of migrants, without a corresponding discussion of who is obligated to protect these rights, risks reducing migrants' rights to empty rhetoric.[14] For example, both the UN Declaration of Human Rights and Pope John XXIII's encyclical *Pacem in terris* (1963) contain thick, substantive lists of positive rights: rights to food, shelter, clean water, employment, health care, education; plus a list of negative rights: the right to be free from slavery, torture, discrimination, and so forth.[15] While the negative rights listed in both documents would easily correlate with a universal duty to refrain from interference in people's freedoms, the positive ones do not lend themselves to universal duties so easily.[16] The idea that every person in the world bears the responsibility to provide positive goods such as food, water, shelter,

---

11. House of Bishops of the Episcopal Church, "The Nation and the Common Good."

12. Kerwin, "Rights, the Common Good," 95.

13. Pope Francis, "Migrants and Refugees: Towards a Better World."

14. Onora O'Neill, *Bounds of Justice* (Cambridge: Cambridge University Press, 2000), 132.

15. United Nations, "The Universal Declaration of Human Rights," December 10, 1948, http://www.un.org/en/documents/udhr/index.shtml. See also Pope John XXIII, *Pacem in terris*, paras. 11–27.

16. Onora O'Neill, *Towards Justice and Virtue: A Constructive Account of Practical Reasoning* (Cambridge: Cambridge University Press, 1996), 129–32.

medical care, and education to every other person in the world is impossible to sustain on any practical level.

Political philosopher Onora O'Neill says that universal positive rights cannot correlate with universal duties because we are finite embodied beings—in her words, "spatially and temporally dispersed." Our attention, time, and material resources are limited. We do not have the "access to one another that universal 'positive' intervention would demand."[17] In other words, our finitude prevents us from being able to provide the goods that universal human rights would demand that we provide to everyone who lacks them. As the saying goes, what is everyone's responsibility becomes no one's responsibility.

If it is insufficient to insist on universal human rights without specifying what persons or institutions have the duty to protect those rights, how do we decide which persons or communities have the obligations to provide for and protect the human rights of others? Many theories of justice presume a world made up of closed nation-states whose citizens do not move around or have relationships with those outside their borders. In such theories, borders themselves can assign specific duties that correlate with universal human rights. In other words, citizens are responsible for providing and protecting the positive rights of one another.[18] The Catholic tradition also insists that the purpose of the nation-state is to protect human rights.[19] Because fellow citizens are often literally our neighbors, and because there are already institutions set up to ensure rights for fellow citizens, this system seems to work quite well much of the time. Every person on earth lives in the territory of some nation-state; every person belongs to a political community that is responsible for guaranteeing his or her human rights.

But the situation of Mario Castro and the millions like him upends the elegance of the nation-state system of guaranteeing human rights. Nation-states often protect the positive human rights of their members; nonmembers are often excluded. Though he was ill and needed heart surgery, Mario Castro could not apply for Medicaid because he was not a US citizen. Though he may have paid Social Security taxes under a counterfeit Social Security number at his restaurant job in California, Castro could not claim disability benefits because he was not a citizen. Castro was not completely excluded from the

---

17. O'Neill, *Towards Justice and Virtue*, 130.

18. Robert Goodin, "What Is So Special about Our Fellow Countrymen?" in *Global Justice: Seminal Essays*, ed. Thomas Pogge and Darrel Moellendorf (St. Paul, MN: Paragon House, 2008).

19. John XXIII, *Pacem in terris*, para. 60.

protection of his human rights; political communities often do protect positive rights even for noncitizens. For example, if Castro had had his family with him in the United States, his children would have had access to both primary and secondary education. However, even when political communities choose to protect the positive rights of nonmembers, noncitizens receive these social goods as a result of the whim of the political community. Their access to these goods cannot be secured because they lack what is perhaps the most important positive right of all: the right to political participation.

Of course, the right to political participation is generally recognized to be a universal human right: it is declared so both in the UN Declaration (Article 21) and in *Pacem in terris* (para. 26). However, this universal right of political participation is a prime example of how it is not enough to insist on human rights without at the same time naming who has the duty to provide for and protect those rights. The right of political participation is surely linked to a universal duty, but whose? The UN Declaration narrows this right by specifying that "Everyone has the right to take part in the government of his country," implying that people do not have the right to take part in the government of another's country. Indeed, it would make little sense to say that everyone has the right to take part in the government of every country or any country in the world. As long as we presume that the world is made up of only closed societies, limiting the right of political participation to one's own government works just fine. However, Mario Castro's situation demonstrates that, if we do not specify which government has the duty to extend opportunities of political participation to which noncitizens, the entire ground of universal human rights becomes shaky indeed.

In other words, while citizens may vote to ensure that their interests are represented by their government, noncitizens are generally not allowed to. Mario Castro is not permitted to participate in shaping society through the democratic process: he may neither vote nor run for office. While he is not legally barred from public speech or protest, such activities, practically speaking, would expose him to the risk of deportation. In the United States, when journalist José Vargas publicly "came out" as an undocumented migrant, he was, in his own words, "risking everything"—his career, his family, and the only home he has known since he was twelve.[20] Many undocumented migrants across the world decide that they cannot take such risks and thus avoid public exposure at all costs.

20. Jose Antonio Vargas, "Vargas: Undocumented and Hiding in Plain Sight," *CNN*, June 30, 2014, http://www.cnn.com/2014/06/26/living/vargas-documented-immigration-essay/.

While US laws do protect Castro and other noncitizens—whether undocumented or not—from workplace exploitation and wage theft, undocumented migrants are not allowed to claim this protection without bringing themselves to the attention of the authorities and risking deportation. Even when migrants are in the territory legally, their presence is based on the whim of the government and not on rights. Ultimately, Castro was deported from the United States and stranded in Mexico; whatever minimal protections he could claim from the US government ended the moment he was deported and no longer under the territorial sovereignty of the United States.

After World War II, Hannah Arendt described the plight of refugees and stateless persons as having lost "the right to have rights."[21] In other words, the loss of a community of people that is responsible for protecting one's rights entails the effective loss of those rights. For Arendt, putative universal human rights are anything but that if a person has no government to protect her. Unlike the refugees and stateless persons who were the subject of Arendt's reflections, economic migrants have not necessarily lost the protection of their governments, but they are living in nation-states not their own. They often have no voice in political processes and secure access to positive human rights.

In essence, Castro and other migrants all over the world lack the fundamental right that secures access to all other rights: they lack the right to be in the territory. Although a Christian ethics of migration can endlessly repeat that migrants have universal human rights, the nation-state system is inadequately structured to protect those rights. Human rights are too closely tied to citizen rights. Noncitizens have no effective way of securing either positive or negative rights, because they are guaranteed access to neither of the two most foundational rights: the right to political participation and the right to remain in the territory.

Although little in Christian ethics of migration directly addresses the problem of who has the responsibility to protect the human rights of migrants, some do offer two implicit solutions for addressing the problem of the asymmetry between human rights and duties. One is to make a world-state or similar international authority responsible for problems of human rights that the nation-state cannot solve. The other is to insist that the nation-state must be responsible for all people within its borders, regardless of their citizenship status. Both of these solutions are explicitly or implicitly cited in various Christian ethics of migration. But both fall short of answering the

---

21. Hannah Arendt, *The Origins of Totalitarianism* (New York: Schocken Books, 2004), 376.

questions about who has responsibility for protecting the human rights of migrants.

The solution of the "worldwide public authority" has a long history in the Catholic tradition. *Pacem in terris*, Pope John XXIII's encyclical about the international order, proposes that in cases where the nation-state cannot or will not protect the rights of those within its borders, a worldwide public authority—the United Nations—is ultimately responsible for protecting a global common good.[22] The vision of the international order outlined in *Pacem in terris* is that, under normal circumstances, citizens will be protected by their own governments. In cases where the national government is unwilling or unable to do so, the worldwide public authority will have the power and the ability to protect not only the human rights of migrants but of all whose governments fail to protect them. However, it is unclear how the worldwide public authority would be able to enforce the rights of migrants and potential migrants who are firmly ensconced inside the borders of countries that are permitted, by virtue of territorial sovereignty, to deport noncitizens who have no right to be there. The principle of territorial sovereignty is almost inviolable in international law, and short of a dramatic revision that gives the worldwide public authority the coercive power to compel nation-states to accept migrants and grant them equal rights with citizens, shifting responsibility to a worldwide public authority will not protect the human rights of migrants. In addition, even if it were possible to endow the worldwide public authority with significant coercive powers, some rights of participation and economic access cannot be guaranteed by an organization as large and unwieldy as a worldwide public authority. In the words of philosopher Kwame Anthony Appiah, "humans live best on the smaller scale."[23] Rights of political, economic, and social participation, such as access to labor and housing markets, might be best secured by nation-states.[24]

In any case, placing responsibility for migrants in the hands of a world public authority also circumvents the question of the responsibilities of native

---

22. Drew Christiansen, "*Pacem in Terris*," in *Modern Catholic Social Teaching: Commentaries and Interpretations*, ed. Kenneth R. Himes et al. (Washington, DC: Georgetown University Press, 2005), 145.

23. Kwame Anthony Appiah, "Cosmopolitan Patriots," in *For Love of Country?* ed. Martha Nussbaum and Joshua Cohen (Boston: Beacon, 1996), 29.

24. This suspicion of a world-state is shared by many political philosophers, e.g., Martha C. Nussbaum, *Frontiers of Justice: Disability, Nationality, Species Membership* (Cambridge, MA: Belknap Press, Harvard University Press, 2006), 313–15; Walzer, *Spheres of Justice*, 29–30.

citizens to migrants. Even if we posit that the worldwide public authority has the protection of human rights as its aim, this does not obviate the question of the responsibilities of states and their citizens. In other words, states still have responsibilities to noncitizens; the worldwide public authority described in *Pacem in terris* may help the state meet those responsibilities, or the worldwide public authority may step in when the state fails in its responsibilities; but the responsibilities of the state and its citizens must be determined independent of the existence and power of a worldwide public authority.

The second way Christian ethicists have tried to respond to the question of who has the duty to protect the human rights of migrants is to link the right of migration to duty: either the duty of states to welcome migrants or the duty of Christians to care for migrants. This marks a departure from many discussions of rights in Christian ethics in which the rights of migrants are decoupled from the duty to protect those rights. Despite the promise of this approach—most clearly laid out in the 2003 pastoral letter of the US and Mexican bishops, entitled "Strangers No Longer"—it risks leaving the protection of human rights to the possibility of benevolent impulses rather than laws and policies.

"Strangers No Longer," for example, upholds both the human right to migrate and the right of states to control their borders, insisting that these two rights "complement" each other.[25] Neither right is absolute. The human right to migrate is based on the teaching of "universal destination of goods," that the goods of the earth were created for the use of all. Thus, when people cannot provide for themselves or their families in their countries of origin, they have a right to migrate (para. 35). The right to migrate as it is described in Catholic social thought is the unlimited right to migrate, as advanced by Joseph Carens, for example.[26] It is rooted in liberal principles of freedom and equality and is only circumscribed by a state's right to secure its borders against real threats.[27]

The right to migrate in order to secure access to goods is linked to the duty of the state to welcome needy migrants where possible (paras. 30, 39). Though "Strangers No Longer" sets out no specific criteria to discern when this duty applies and when it does not, it is linked to the ultimate purpose of the state: to uphold the common good (para. 39). For the US and Mexican

---

25. United States Conference of Catholic Bishops and Conferencia del Episcopado Mexicano, "Strangers No Longer: Together on the Journey of Hope," paras. 35–36, 39. Hereafter, paragraph numbers for this document appear in parentheses within the text.

26. Carens, *The Ethics of Immigration*.

27. Carens, *The Ethics of Immigration*, chap. 11.

bishops, borders serve an important function in creating and maintaining conditions of political stability. Arguably, states need to regulate immigration for a variety of reasons: to protect the political community from terrorists, to ensure that social service agencies do not become overwhelmed with newcomers (para. 39), and, in some cases, to protect the community from colonization by immigration.[28] The state thus has a duty to welcome migrants whenever it can do so without compromising its ability to protect the common good. The bishops put it this way:

> In the current condition of the world, in which global poverty and persecution are rampant, the presumption is that persons must migrate in order to support and protect themselves and that the nations who are able to receive them should accommodate this right. (para. 39)

If the US and Mexican bishops were to apply these two rights to the situation of Mario Castro, they would conclude that the United States would have had an obligation to admit Mario Castro—in accordance with his right to migrate. Because Castro posed no security threat to the United States, because the United States is a wealthy country that can easily provide both employment and medical care for him, and because Castro has a legitimate need to both provide for his family and to secure medical care for his illness, he fits into the category of those who should be admitted. Once Castro was in the United States, the US society would have an obligation to protect Castro's human rights by protecting him against workplace exploitation. In other words, according to "Strangers No Longer," Castro should never have become an undocumented migrant and thus should never have been deported. Because of his great need, he should have been admitted to the territory legally.

The solution offered by such accounts has much merit. In the words of Karen Lebacqz, these situations are not merely unfortunate, they are unfair.[29] The bishops underscore the fundamental unfairness of Castro's predicament. In presenting an ideal in which every migrant is admitted and protected on the basis of need, they show how far wealthy countries are falling short of their responsibilities to migrants. However, despite the contributions of this approach, in the final analysis it leaves migrants in a precarious position in that no state or community is fully responsible for protecting the full spectrum of their rights.

---

28. This point comes from a personal conversation with Daniel Kanstroom.

29. Karen Lebacqz, *Justice in an Unjust World: Foundations for a Christian Approach to Justice* (Minneapolis: Augsburg, 1987), 7.

The first problem is that, like many Christian ethics of migration, "Strangers No Longer" ultimately maintains a moral distinction between citizens and migrants. Although they circumscribe the right of the state to control its borders, the bishops stop short of insisting that migrants have the right to citizenship. The distinction between legal permanent residency and full citizenship might seem merely academic, but only full citizenship guarantees the full rights of political participation and residency. Without full citizenship, Mario Castro could not secure the all-important right of full political participation. And though "Strangers No Longer" only implies this without stating it explicitly, responsibilities to migrants without full citizenship remain less than responsibilities to full citizens. In the abstract, states can refuse to admit migrants and thus protect their human rights in defense of the common good; however, states can never disavow their responsibilities to protect the human rights of their own citizens. In other works, the difference between responsibilities to fellow citizens and to migrants is particularly pronounced.

This is the case in Pope John Paul II's "World Day of Migration" (1996) message, in which he encourages all Christians to help undocumented migrants legalize their status. That statement asserts, however, that if the laws of the state do not permit this, Christians should help undocumented migrants "to seek acceptance in other countries or to return to their own country."[30] While Christians would presumably be urged to care for and provide for vulnerable fellow citizens without qualification, Christians are responsible to undocumented migrants only if they can work within the laws of their country. Otherwise, undocumented migrants might be deported to other countries where they might find themselves beyond the responsibility of these Christians. Though many other Christian ethicists are far more skeptical of the justness of the laws of any nation-state than John Paul II appears to be, few Christian ethicists address whether and why responsibilities for migrants should be the same as responsibilities to fellow citizens.

The reluctance to insist on full membership for migrants implies that responsibilities to fellow citizens are stronger than responsibilities to strangers—except possibly in cases when the migrants are exceptionally needy. Others in the world are just as needy or more needy than Mario Castro is. In order for the bishops to insist that migrants in the territory or at the border have stronger claims on citizens, there needs to be some criterion of

---

30. Pope John Paul II, "Undocumented Migrants."

proximity or ability to help at play in this document. But the bishops never explicitly name it.

The second problem is that, in failing to insist that migrants have rights to citizenship, "Strangers No Longer" falls prey to a tendency to make the humane treatment of migrants a matter of supererogatory benevolence rather than a matter of justice—that is, what is *owed* to migrants. The policy recommendations that follow in "Strangers No Longer," for example, policies that would reduce the number of undocumented migrants, are consistently presented as something that would benefit both migrants and the host country. In other words, the legalization of undocumented migrants is never presented as something owed to migrants; rather, it is presented as a practical solution for the host country. In asymmetrically affirming the rights of nation-states to control their borders without spelling out the duties of citizens to migrants, "Strangers No Longer" risks leaving the protection of the human rights of migrants to the self-interested and only possibly benevolent impulses of citizens.

The asymmetrical insistence on the human rights of migrants without designation of who has the responsibility to protect these rights is mirrored in policy imperatives that urge that the "root causes" of migration be addressed so that people do not have to migrate in the first place.[31] Catholic social thought on migration takes these root causes to be poverty and inequality in the countries of origin. Of course, migration should ideally be the result of free choice rather than desperation. However, the imperative is without an agent. Who should address the root causes of migration? Wealthy countries? Countries that the migrants have left? The international community? Without a specification of who bears the responsibility to address these root causes and why, it is difficult to see how migrants have any claim on any particular political community.

The Limitations of the Preferential Option for the Poor

"Strangers No Longer" implies that migrants have a special claim to protection because their status as noncitizens makes them especially vulnerable. In making society responsible for the human rights of those who are most likely to have their rights violated, the document implicitly draws on what

---

31. "Strangers No Longer," para. 57; Gustavo Gutiérrez, "Poverty, Migration, and the Option for the Poor," in Groody and Campese, *A Promised Land*, 81.

theologians call the preferential option for the poor: the idea that God, as he is revealed in Scripture, consistently chooses to be on the side of the poor, the marginalized, and the oppressed. This biblical concern for the poor, orphans, widows, and strangers reverses our all-too-human tendency to keep our eyes on the rich and powerful because, by virtue of their wealth and power, they command more of our attention. Just as God "opts" for the poor, Christians should act in defense of the poor—in this case, the vulnerable migrants who live in desperate poverty at the margins of society. Thus, while "Strangers No Longer" does not explicitly invoke the option for the poor, the document repeatedly reminds readers that migrants are among the most powerless and vulnerable in society. A similar move has been made by many other Christian ethicists and theologians. More recently, Pope Francis castigated the European Union for allowing the Mediterranean to become a "graveyard" for migrants, reflecting Francis's own commitment to the option for the poor.[32] Here the option for the poor functions as a mandate to resist the "globalization of indifference" to the suffering and deaths of migrants and refugees.[33]

The option for the poor is explicitly named in the ethics of migration of more radical Christian ethicists, who insist that citizens have the same obligations to migrants and potential migrants that they do to fellow citizens. Unlike the direction taken in "Strangers No Longer," these theologians and ethicists are explicit about the fact that migrants have a claim on citizens precisely because they are needy and vulnerable. In his 2009 essay "Poverty, Migration, and the Option for the Poor," Gustavo Gutiérrez draws on the parable of the Good Samaritan in order to claim that, just as the Samaritan assisted the wounded Jew on the side of the road, Christians must help their poorest and most vulnerable neighbors. Since the parable ends with Jesus's instruction to "go and do likewise" (Luke 10:37), we, too, must make ourselves the neighbor of migrants. Differences of language, culture, and ethnicity mean nothing in the face of the gospel mandate to make ourselves the neighbors of the poor and vulnerable in our midst. William O'Neill makes a similar argument when he links the parable of the Good Samaritan to fundamental human rights: the virtue of hospitality, as illustrated in the para-

32. Ian Traynor, "Pope Francis attacks EU over treatment of immigrants," *The Guardian*, November 25, 2014, http://www.theguardian.com/world/2014/nov/25/pope-francis-elderly-eu-lost-bearings.

33. Pope Francis, homily, Lampedusa, Italy, July 8, 2013, http://w2.vatican.va/content/francesco/en/homilies/2013/documents/papa-francesco_20130708_omelia-lampedusa.html.

ble, entails recognizing and protecting the human rights of the migrant.[34] Pope Francis has invoked the same parable as a reproach to those who, like the Levite and priest, deny their responsibility to vulnerable migrants and refugees.[35]

The centrality of the option for the poor in a Christian ethics of migration has much to recommend it: it is a radical step that makes poverty and vulnerability themselves the basis of stronger Christian responsibilities. Although Pope Francis does not say so explicitly, the migrants who, in their desperation to reach Europe, perish in the Mediterranean are forgotten precisely because they are migrants.[36] Just as they have no political community willing to protect their human rights, they also often have no community willing to remember their suffering and often their deaths. Grounded in the option for the poor, Pope Francis's call to weep for these migrants is a powerful call to include migrants in the responsibilities that bind people together in a society. The option for the poor has a prophetic force in societies determined to see neither the humanity of migrants nor the claims that such humanity has on all of us.

While the ethics of universal human rights most often assumes that there is a nation-state or some other kind of institutional structure to protect human rights, the preferential option for the poor can be taken up not only by governments, but also by institutions of all kinds as well as individuals. Although the option for the poor would seem, because of its grounding in Scripture, to speak exclusively to Christians, it can also speak persuasively to secular audiences. For example, when Pope Francis makes public proclamations invoking the option for the poor, he is not necessarily addressing Christians exclusively. Many people who are not Christian can hear the pope's call to see the suffering of migrants and have compassion for them. The call to weep for migrants can speak to individuals, communities, and perhaps even entire societies. This appeal to the affective dimension of human experience reveals the role of compassion in working for policy changes at the institutional level. If individuals, churches, and societies do not weep for migrants, there is no chance that political institutions will change.

The option for the poor is fundamental to any Christian ethics of migration. However, when it is used in isolation from a larger account of responsi-

---

34. William O'Neill, "Christian Hospitality and Solidarity with the Stranger," in Kerwin and Gerschutz, *And You Welcomed Me.*

35. Pope Francis, homily, Lampedusa, Italy.

36. Pope Francis, homily, Lampedusa, Italy.

bility, the option for the poor has similar shortcomings to an approach that is based on universal human rights. Without assigning who has the duty to opt for which groups of impoverished and vulnerable people, the option for the poor fails to account for why a particular group of people should take responsibility for a particular group of needy and vulnerable poor. For example, when Mario Castro was an undocumented migrant living and working in California, he was among the poorest and most vulnerable in the United States. By virtue of his poverty, illness, and status as a noncitizen, the option for the poor suggests that he should have had a preferential claim on the resources of the citizens of California and the United States. So far, this is an appealing solution to the question of responsibilities to migrants: citizens are responsible to migrants by virtue of their very poverty and vulnerability. However, this neat solution to the question of responsibility is complicated by the fact that, by the time Margaret Regan told Castro's story, he had already been deported to Mexico, a country where he was also a migrant. Who, then, bears responsibility for Castro? The citizens of the United States, the citizens of Mexico, or the citizens of Guatemala? If the basis of the option for the poor is need and vulnerability, why would Castro, stranded in Mexico, have a greater claim than his neighbors in Guatemala City—those who could not afford even to migrate?

Perhaps the option for the poor works best for migrants who are already in a particular political community. Then, as political philosopher Robert Goodin suggests, the border itself becomes what assigns responsibilities to individuals and institutions, not because borders create differences in the moral worth of individuals but because borders are a convenient, though historically arbitrary, way to assign moral responsibility.[37] However, as the plight of Mario Castro reveals, Goodin's simple solution fails when we consider those who are neither here nor there, those stranded in the borderlands. In addition, though Goodin insists that borders are morally arbitrary, his argument does give borders a practical weight in assigning responsibilities for human rights. Some recent Christian ethical reflections on migration call into question whether borders should bear such a weight at all, and whether Christian theology in fact challenges the moral legitimacy of borders.[38]

---

37. Goodin, "What Is So Special about Our Fellow Countrymen?" 255–84.

38. Marianne Heimbach-Steins, "The Ambivalence of Borders and the Challenge of an Ethics of Liminality," in *Living with(out) Borders*, ed. Agnes M. Brazal and María T. Dávila (Maryknoll, NY: Orbis, 2016).

Nor does Goodin's solution help sort through responsibilities to the poor who are outside the territory, such as Castro's family and neighbors who remain in Guatemala City. What responsibilities do we have to those who are every bit as poor and vulnerable as the migrants in our midst, but who live across the border—or across the world? Christian migration ethicists who invoke the option for the poor for migrants do have their own way of bringing attention to the plight of would-be migrants in the developing world. They insist that poverty and inequality are the driving factors of migration: that is, they are part of the structural sin that marks the global economic system, in which some countries enjoy health and wealth, while others are plagued by poverty and death. Gustavo Gutiérrez, for example, writes that addressing the causes of poverty is inseparable from a theology of migration, presumably because under this macro-neoclassical theory of migration (see chapter 2), poverty itself causes migration.[39] In his message for the 2014 World Migration Day, Pope Francis follows the same line of reasoning, linking poverty to migration.[40] If migration is the result of poverty, perhaps nation-states would be responsible not only for the vulnerable migrants within their borders but also for the structural causes of migration, including poverty in other lands. In fact, this is the very reasoning behind the policy recommendations of "Strangers No Longer," which insists that reducing poverty in countries of emigration will reduce the number of people who are driven to migrate in the first place.[41]

However, migration theorists have long argued that migration is not driven solely by poverty, unemployment, and economic inequality. In fact, it is not the poorest of the world who tend to migrate; indeed, the poorest countries have relatively low rates of emigration.[42] In addition, of course, the very poorest in the emigration countries are usually unable to save the tens of thousands of dollars required to migrate. Furthermore, the evidence of migration theory suggests that it is by no means clear that developing foreign economies will halt migration; much of the data suggests that foreign aid can, under some circumstances, actually increase migration rates.[43] In other words, although using the preferential option for the poor as a central principle for a Christian ethics of migration does direct our attention

39. Gutiérrez, "Poverty, Migration, and the Option for the Poor," 81.

40. Pope Francis, "Migrants and Refugees."

41. "Strangers No Longer," paras. 59–61.

42. Ronald Skeldon, *Migration and Development: A Global Perspective* (London: Addison-Wesley Longman Higher Education, 1997), 8.

43. Skeldon, *Migration and Development*, 8.

both to the plight of migrants worldwide and to the real vulnerability of migrants in our midst, the option for the poor does not by itself help us sort through our competing responsibilities to citizens, migrants, and potential migrants—both near and far.

Perhaps the theologians and ethicists who emphasize the option for the poor would respond that it is not meant to be a heuristic for sorting through competing responsibilities. Instead, it is meant as a theological proclamation that those who are most often ignored and mistreated are in fact the heirs to the kingdom of God. While such theological proclamations must be central to any Christian ethics of migration, they are by themselves not up to the task of discerning how to instantiate these theological values in historical, particular communities made up of embodied, finite people and communities.

A New Approach

Neither universal human rights nor the option for the poor is sufficient by itself to help sort through competing responsibilities to fellow human beings, both migrants and citizens, both those who reside close to us and those far away. At a time when the rise of white nationalist groups in the United States and Europe has become a serious threat to the human rights of migrants, few Christian ethicists would seriously claim that migrants are not people, endowed with rights by virtue of their being human rather than their being citizens. Nor is it disputed that migrants are needy and vulnerable humans. The contribution of liberation theology to the field of Christian ethics is such that no Christian ethicist would look at the plight of migrants such as Mario Castro and disagree that, by virtue of his poverty, illness, and lack of citizenship in either the United States or Mexico, he is in a most vulnerable situation, and that his very need gives him great claims on both Christians and their larger political communities. While Christian ethicists have made enormous contributions to the ethics of migration by placing human rights and the option for the poor at the center of the discussions, in order to prevent universal human rights and the option for the poor from becoming empty rhetoric, Christian ethics must address this pressing question: Who has the responsibility to protect the rights of poor and vulnerable migrants?

While Goodin offers one criterion—the criterion of who is inside the border—David Hollenbach offers another set of criteria by proposing to apply the "Kew Gardens Principle" as an answer to the question of who has the responsibility to defend and protect the human rights of refugees.[44] Derived from a case study in which a woman was murdered while bystanders looked on and did nothing, the Kew Gardens Principle suggests that bystanders have the responsibility to intervene (a) when the need is great; (b) when the bystanders are in close proximity to the need; (c) when the bystanders have the ability to help; and (d) when the needy person can look to no one else for help.[45] Hollenbach argues that these criteria taken together indicate that the "rich countries of the developed world" have both the proximity (which he interprets here not only as geographical proximity but as knowledge of the situation at hand) and the capabilities to help refugees in great need. One possible solution to our central question would be to take Hollenbach's argument of the Kew Gardens Principle and apply it to the situation of Mario Castro and other economic migrants. The question of who has the responsibility to protect human rights and provide for a particular group of poor and vulnerable people could be answered thus: by whoever has knowledge of the need and the capability to help, presumably wealthy nations who are already hosting migrants. This is, in fact, strikingly similar to the implicit account of responsibility offered by "Strangers No Longer."

However, the Kew Gardens Principle is inappropriate for an ethics of economic migration—and perhaps inappropriate to protect the rights of many refugees—for this reason: economic migrants are not, in fact, strangers to citizens. Hollenbach himself says that the Kew Gardens Principle was developed "to help identify when persons have duties to remedy harms *that they have not themselves caused.*"[46] In fact, the bystanders in the murder were strangers to the young woman. Similarly, both Gutiérrez and O'Neill retell the parable of the Good Samaritan as a parable in which acts of compassion turn a vulnerable stranger into a neighbor.[47] In both Hollenbach's appropriation of the Kew Gardens Principle and Gutiérrez's and O'Neill's application of the Good Samaritan parable, citizens are to migrants as bystanders are to strangers.

But the analogy of citizens to previously uninvolved strangers and migrants to wounded strangers is an inaccurate analogy. There are many ways

---

44. David Hollenbach, "Internally Displaced People, Sovereignty, and the Responsibility to Protect," in Hollenbach, *Refugee Rights: Ethics, Advocacy, and Africa* (Washington, DC: Georgetown University Press, 2008).

45. Hollenbach, "Internally Displaced People," 188.

46. Hollenbach, "Internally Displaced People," 188 (emphasis added).

47. Gutiérrez, "Poverty, Migration, and the Option for the Poor"; see also William O'Neill, "Christian Hospitality and Solidarity with the Stranger."

of studying and understanding migration, and only a minority of theorists would describe economic migration as the arrival of previously unknown strangers in search of new homes. Instead, specific kinds of relationships drive migration. Understanding these relationships is the key to developing an account of justice that can respond to the central question of who has the responsibility to protect the human rights of migrants.

For Further Reading

The 2003 encyclical of the US and Mexican Bishops, "Strangers No Longer," sums up a Catholic position on the ethics of migration. Donald Kerwin and Jill Marie Gerschutz's edited collection *And You Welcomed Me: Migration and Catholic Social Thought* (Lanham, MD: Lexington Books, 2009) contains helpful explications of the themes in "Strangers No Longer."

Two recent book-length treatments of a Christian ethics of migration are Kristin Heyer's *Kinship across Borders: A Christian Ethic of Immigration* (Washington, DC: Georgetown University Press, 2012) and Ilsup Ahn's *Religious Ethics and Migration* (New York: Routledge, 2014). Heyer writes from a Catholic perspective and Ahn from a Protestant perspective.

Living with(out) Borders: Catholic Theological Ethics on the Migration of Peoples, edited by Agnes M. Brazal and María T. Dávila (Maryknoll, NY: Orbis, 2016), is a collection of diverse theological and ethical perspectives on international migration from a Catholic perspective.

Two edited collections on the human rights of refugees are David Hollenbach's *Refugee Rights: Ethics, Advocacy, and Africa* (Washington, DC: Georgetown University Press, 2008) and *Driven from Home: Protecting the Rights of Forced Migrants* (Washington, DC: Georgetown University Press, 2010).

For an incisive critique of human rights discourse, see Onora O'Neill's *Justice across Boundaries: Whose Obligations?* esp. chap. 12, "The Dark Side of Human Rights" (Cambridge: Cambridge University Press, 2016).

CHAPTER 2

Migration Theory and Migration Ethics

Enrique's Journey, a 2006 work of nonfiction by journalist Sonia Nazario, is the story of seventeen-year-old Enrique, who sets off alone from Honduras in search of his mother, who had left her family and community and made the arduous and perilous journey to the United States because of the crushing poverty of her family.[1] Unable to find a job in Honduras that would allow her to send her children to school or even feed them, she had set out for the United States and eventually settled in North Carolina. Twelve years later, Enrique follows in his mother's path, leaving behind his pregnant girlfriend and his extended family. Although he intends to work only briefly in the United States before returning to his family, Enrique remains with this mother in North Carolina. Soon Enrique's girlfriend follows Enrique, leaving their young daughter with relatives in Honduras in hopes that she can send for her daughter when she is able.

The story of Enrique and his family is hardly unique. Enrique's mother becomes one of millions of undocumented migrant women hoping to be able to support her family through remittances. Enrique is only one of hundreds of thousands of children who risk life and limb to reunite with their mothers in the United States. In Nazario's account, both Enrique and his mother leave Honduras because of the promise of a better life in the United States. Similarly, Margaret Regan's stories of dozens of migrants who brave death in the Arizona desert report again and again that migrants leave home because they cannot provide for their families in their home countries. Regan's implication is that only migrants in utterly desperate situations would risk the dangers of the journey through the desert. Both Nazario and Regan present

---

1. Sonia Nazario, *Enrique's Journey: The Story of a Boy's Dangerous Odyssey to Reunite with His Mother* (New York: Random House, 2014).

migration as the only reasonable choice that migrants can make in the face of desperate poverty and high unemployment.

Migration theorists, armed with the disciplinary tools of sociology, demography, history, and economics, often understand the causes of migration quite differently. They often theorize that poverty and unemployment only partially account for the factors that drive migration. In the first two chapters of this book I pose a central question: Who is responsible for protecting the human rights of migrants? I suggest that, in order to answer this question, we must understand migration "in its complex and multifaceted totality."[2] Migration theorist Saskia Sassen writes:

> If immigration is thought of as the result of the aggregation of individuals in search of a better life, immigration is, from the perspective of the receiving country, an exogenous process, one formed and shaped by conditions outside the receiving country. The receiving country is then saddled with the task of accommodating this population. . . . The receiving country's experience is understood to be that of a passive bystander to processes outside its domain and control, and hence with few options but tight closing of frontiers if it is to avoid an "invasion."[3]

In other words, if we understand migration to be the result of poverty and desperation, then we will think that the host country bears either the responsibility for defending its borders or for generously accommodating the impoverished masses. Either way, the receiving country is a "passive bystander" to forces beyond its control. However, if we understand migration as Sassen and other migration-systems theorists argue we should, receiving countries will have to come to a new way of understanding migration and their role in it.

I argue that Christian ethicists must think about migration in a new way, one that places poverty and unemployment within the context of larger historical, political, and social factors. This new way of thinking about migration will more accurately reflect both Christian anthropological assumptions about the relationality of humans and the most current insights of migration theorists.

There is no universal theory of migration. The field of migration theory is interdisciplinary, drawing on the methodological insights from the fields

2. Gioacchino Campese, "Beyond Ethnic and National Imagination," in Hondagneu-Sotelo, *Religion and Social Justice for Immigrants*, 180.

3. Saskia Sassen, *Guests and Aliens* (New York: New Press, 1999), 136.

of economics, sociology, demography, and history. Migration theory, like every other academic field, is marked by diversity and disagreement. Current migration theorists disagree with theorists of the past; and, of course, contemporary migration theorists disagree with each other. Still, it is possible for Christian ethicists to evaluate migration theories. The field of Christian ethics can contribute anthropological insights—insights about the nature of the human person and human societies—to discussions of migration theory. For example, most migration theories present humans as either choosing agents isolated to a greater or lesser degree from their larger social, political, or economic contexts, or they neglect the agency of humans in an effort to focus on the larger structures that drive migration. Christian ethicist Margaret Farley, on the other hand, suggests a view of the person having an autonomy that functions only in relationship to other people.[4] Her account of autonomy-in-relation suggests that humans can be reduced to neither autonomous rational agents nor mere victims of social structures beyond their control. I argue that Christian ethicists must use migration theories that pay attention to both the agency of migrants and the larger context in which migrants make decisions for themselves and their families.

I cite the story of Enrique and his family to present different kinds of migration theories: agency-dominant migration theories; structure-dominant migration theories; and migration-systems theories.

Agency-dominant migration theories present an account of migration from the perspective of the migrants as choosing agents. This is the perspective adopted by many Christian ethicists and policy-makers alike, regardless of the ethical and policy directives they ultimately adopt.

Structure-dominant theories of migration focus on the larger structural forces that drive migration, including labor markets and economic policies of receiving countries. This perspective is neglected by many views of the ethics of migration. However, it is not sufficient by itself to fully explain the phenomenon of migration because it omits the voices and experiences of migrants themselves.

Migration-systems theory is an alternative to both agency-dominant and structure-dominant theories of migration. This theory accounts for both human agency and social structures by describing migrant agency as operating in the context of social structures. Certain kinds of social structures are in turn created and changed by the agency of migrants. Migration theory thus

---

4. Margaret A. Farley, "A Feminist Version of Respect for Persons," *Journal of Feminist Studies in Religion* 9, nos. 1–2 (Spring–Fall 1993): 183–98.

assumes a relational account of human agency, in which decisions about migration are always made in a social, historical, and political context.

Migration Theory and Christian Ethics: Possibilities and Limitations[5]

Before embarking on this review of migration theory, we must observe some definitions of terms and scope. Migration theory is a broad term that includes theories concerning many aspects of human migration. Here I consider only those migration theories that describe what Stephen Castles and Mark Miller term "the determinants, processes, and patterns of migration."[6] Why and how do people migrate? Why do migrants go to one country and not another? Left aside are migration theories of immigrant incorporation, which address how immigrants settle into their new countries.

When reviewing and assessing migration theories, we must keep in mind that no one theory has the consensus of all migration theorists. This is partly because the empirical data do not conclusively support one theory over others,[7] and in part because empirical researchers are often not concerned with trying to prove one theory over another.[8] Some migration theorists even caution against trying to find a universal theory of migration, arguing that any such theory risks being too vague or general to be helpful.[9] Despite these cautions, there are at least two reasons that Christian ethicists must use migration theory.

First of all, avoiding any generalizations about migration at all leaves ethicists without any way to understand migration. As Gioacchino Campese points out, Christian ethicists cannot make normative statements about migration without understanding the reality of migration.[10] Migration theories

5. Some of this material appears in Rajendra, "Justice, Not Benevolence: Catholic Social Thought, Migration Theory, and the Rights of Migrants," *Political Theology* 15, no. 3 (2014): 290–306.

6. Stephen Castles and Mark J. Miller, *The Age of Migration: International Population Movements in the Modern World*, 4th ed. (New York: Guilford, 2009), 20.

7. Joaquin Arango, "Explaining Migration: A Critical View," *International Social Science Journal* 52, no. 3 (2000): 283–96.

8. Arango, "Explaining Migration," 295.

9. See, e.g., Alejandro Portes, "Immigration Theory for a New Century: Some Problems and Opportunities," *International Migration Review* 31, no. 4 (1997): 810.

10. Campese, "Beyond Ethnic and National Imagination," 180.

can help Christian ethicists understand part of this reality, as long as they keep in mind that these theories will constantly be revised as new empirical data come to light. Secondly, as we have seen, even when they do not explicitly draw on migration theory, Christian ethicists make assumptions about how migration works whenever they make normative statements about migration. Rather than risk making inaccurate assumptions about migration, Christian ethicists must deliberately use migration theory in order to make better and more humble generalizations about migration, always remaining attentive to developments in the field of migration theory.

One way to use migration theory while remaining aware of the limitations of such theories is to use "middle-range theories," which seek to explain similar kinds of migration.[11] In other words, instead of chasing a grand migration theory that attempts to explain all human movement, we can, with the judicious use of middle-range theories, make sense of patterns that emerge in certain kinds of migration: for example, internal rural-urban migration in developing countries, or labor migration from South Asia to the Middle East. For this reason I focus on labor migration from developing countries to Western democracies. The migration theories I discuss here address these kinds of migration. While the ethical issues surrounding transnational migration are manifold, I am especially drawn to migrants who are particularly vulnerable to exploitation and abuse because of their relative poverty and lack of education. These migrants are particularly harmed by inaccurate understandings of migration theory.

Agency-Dominant Theories of Migration

Agency-dominant accounts of migration, neoclassical migration theory and the new economics of migration, are rooted in the discipline of economics. These theories, which focus on the migrant as a rational, choosing agent, are also the dominant accounts of migration in the public square. Such theories assume that a migrant in search of a country is like a worker in search of a job.[12] A potential migrant evaluates what she might gain or lose by migrating and chooses to leave her country of origin if the potential gains outweigh the

---

11. See, e.g., Stephen Castles, "Understanding Global Migration: A Social Transformational Perspective," *Journal of Ethnic and Migration Studies* 36, no. 10 (2010): 1572.

12. George J. Borjas, *Friends or Strangers: The Impact of Immigrants on the U.S. Economy* (New York: Basic Books, 1990), 12.

potential losses. In countries where poverty is rampant and economic opportunities are few, people are more likely to emigrate because the potential gains are much more likely to outweigh the potential losses.

Neoclassical migration theory draws on the premises of neoclassical economics: that persons are rational, self-interested actors in pursuit of the maximization of their utility. The migrant in neoclassical migration theory is thus a completely rational actor who is motivated by economic incentives. Neoclassical migration theory would understand Enrique's family's migration by highlighting the fact that Enrique's mother, Lourdes, left Honduras because she could make more money in the United States. Whereas she could barely afford to feed her children in Honduras, her wages in the United States were high enough that she could not only support herself but could also, from time to time, have extra money that would allow her to send toys and school supplies to Enrique and his sister back in Honduras.[13] According to neoclassical migration theory, inequality in wages—the most easily quantifiable measure of well-being—represents the primary factor driving migration. Wage inequalities are impacted by the inequalities of supply and demand in labor markets in the host country and the country of origin. Wherever there is a large pool of low-wage laborers, but no jobs, migration will follow. Migration can also be driven by conditions in the country of origin, such as poverty, unemployment, and political instability, since such factors make it more likely that people will have much to gain from migrating.

In the field of migration theory, neoclassical approaches to migration have largely fallen out of favor, due in large part to the fact that they cannot explain much of the empirical data. For one thing, neoclassical migration theory predicts that migration would occur any time wage differentials exist between two countries, and this is simply not the case. Other migration theorists point out that, even in countries where emigration rates are very high, emigrants are only a tiny fraction of a country's overall population; the neoclassical model would predict, on the contrary, that anyone who can gain economically from migrating would do so.[14] Furthermore, neoclassical migration theory predicts that the very poorest in the world, those who have the most to gain, would be the most likely to migrate. But the evidence does not bear that out either.[15] The world's poorest people do not migrate. Lastly, though they purport to explain why people migrate, neoclassical migration

---

13. Nazario, *Enrique's Journey*, 9.
14. Sassen, *Guests and Aliens*, 141.
15. Skeldon, *Migration and Development*, 8.

theorists cannot explain where migrants go. Such theories cannot explain why North Africans, for example, tend to migrate to France rather than Canada, or why Mexicans generally go to the United States instead of Germany. Neoclassical migration theory would predict that there would be movement whenever there is economic inequality between any two countries; but, in fact, many countries have large wage differentials but no migration between them.[16]

Another reason that neoclassical migration theory has fallen out of favor is that migration theorists came to reject neoclassical migration theory's premise that migrants are rational actors who make fully informed decisions.[17] In this theory, migrants are solely autonomous rational agents acting outside the concerns or constraints of family, community, and history. With all the information they need to make informed choices about migration, they make decisions concerning their own well-being without regard for anyone else. Even a cursory examination of Enrique's story reveals the flaws in neoclassical migration theory. Lourdes makes the decision to migrate, not to maximize her own economic well-being, but that of her family. Lourdes's abject poverty is not only the result of high unemployment in Honduras; she is subject to the economic vulnerability of single mothers (her husband had abandoned her for another woman). While Lourdes's decisions are economically motivated (though not self-interested), Enrique's decisions are not. Like Lourdes, he does want to secure a job once he arrives in the United States and wants to be able to send money to his family back in Honduras; but he is quite clear that his primary motivation for making the journey is to find his mother, whom he has not seen in twelve years. Enrique idolizes his absent mother and thinks that their reunion holds the key to resolving his feelings of abandonment.[18] The economic motives for Enrique, a young man of seventeen, are entirely secondary. Enrique persists in his quest to reach his mother even as he is deported from Mexico time after time, even as he is attacked by bandits, even as he watches other migrants lose their lives or limbs as they are tossed from the train traveling through Central America and into Mexico. Enrique's drive to reunite with his mother cannot be explained by the maximization of utility.

Neither Lourdes nor Enrique makes decisions that are fully informed.

16. Douglas S. Massey et al., *Worlds in Motion: Understanding International Migration at the End of the Millennium* (Oxford: Oxford University Press, 2005), 8.

17. Jon Goss and Bruce Lindquist, "Conceptualizing International Labor Migration: A Structuration Perspective," *International Migration Review* 29, no. 2 (1995): 320.

18. Nazario, *Enrique's Journey*, 42.

Once Lourdes arrives in the United States, she finds herself still living in poverty. She is reluctant to bring her children to her drug- and crime-infested neighborhood in Los Angeles.[19] When Enrique sets out to join her, he does not know the dangers that are in store for him on the journey. In other words, it is impossible to accurately describe the mother's and son's decisions to migrate using neoclassical migration theory.

Another agency-dominant theory of migration, the new economics of migration, was developed in response to these criticisms of neoclassical migration theory. This theory proposes that people migrate to maximize not their own utility but that of their families and communities. Rather than seeing Lourdes and Enrique as atomized individuals, the new economics of migration would see them as embedded within their nuclear and extended families. This theory would highlight the fact that both Lourdes and Enrique migrate in order to provide for their children. Their decision is made possible only because their extended families agree to care for children while they are gone.

The new economics of migration also expands the definition of economic well-being, which is not only a matter of wages but also of security and participation in community. Migration is thus driven not only by low wages or unemployment; lack of insurance against crop failures in agricultural communities, lack of access to credit, the absence of national pension or social security plans and unemployment insurance—all these leave families and communities unprotected against both natural and man-made disasters.[20] Had Lourdes been a single mother in a country with a strong social-welfare system and generous support for single mothers, she might not have needed to migrate. But with none of these provisions for her to fall back on, migration enables her to provide for her children and her extended family. In many countries of emigration, the few family members who work abroad function as a kind of insurance against a sudden loss of livelihood. Accordingly, migration ensures much more than the maximization of individual utility; migration can insulate entire families and communities against financial catastrophe.

Although the new economics of migration improves on the radical individualism of neoclassical migration theory, both of these theories tend to focus on the agency of migrants apart from the larger forces that may drive migration. Neoclassical migration theory is particularly egregious in

19. Nazario, *Enrique's Journey*, 23.
20. Massey et al., *Worlds in Motion*, 22–26.

reducing humans to rational, self-interested agents disconnected from the ties of family, language, history, culture, and place. These agents act in a cultural and historical vacuum, merely out of economic self-interest rather than commitments to other people or to values.[21] While the new economics of migration understands the migrant as embedded in a family and community, its understanding of the agent as driven by the maximization of utility—this time of a community rather than an individual—remains.

This assumption of the primacy of rationality is rooted in a certain kind of liberalism, in which persons are defined solely by their capacity to rationally choose their own ends—a notion that is much criticized by feminist[22] and communitarian ethicists.[23] These imagined autonomous agents are isolated from not only their social ties, values, history, tradition, and community, but also from the political and economic context of their decisions. Neither the immigration policies nor the dynamics of labor markets in receiving countries, for example, play any part in these theories, except as they impact the cost-benefit analysis of each potential migrant. In other words, everything in the migrant's experience can be filtered through a calculation of utility.

However, if we reduce migrants (or any group of people) to the level of self-interested rational agents, we miss key insights about who and what these people are. Feminist theologians and ethicists have consistently pointed to the ways in which this assumption of autonomous rational agency has hampered philosophical and theological discussions of justice.[24] Feminist ethicists such as Margaret Farley have suggested that, while people certainly possess capacities of rationality and autonomy, they use those capacities in a social context in which they are bound to others. Therefore, when María Isabel, Enrique's girlfriend, decides to leave their three-year-old daughter with relatives in Honduras to join Enrique in the United States, she reasons that her daughter will benefit in the long run. She weighs the prospects of marrying another man in Honduras, someone who will never accept her daughter as his own, against joining Enrique in the United States, where she can send for her daughter once she gets established. She believes that

---

21. Amartya Sen, "Rational Fools: A Critique of the Behavioral Foundations of Economic Theory," *Philosophy and Public Affairs* 6, no. 4 (1977): 317–44.

22. See, e.g., Alison M. Jaggar, *Feminist Politics and Human Nature*, Philosophy and Society 1 (Totowa, NJ: Rowman and Allanheld, 1983), 44–45.

23. See, e.g., Michael J. Sandel, *Liberalism and the Limits of Justice*, 2nd ed. (Cambridge: Cambridge University Press, 1998).

24. See Sandra Sullivan Dunbar, *Human Dependency and Christian Ethics* (Cambridge: Cambridge University Press, 2017).

the pain of separation will be easier for her daughter to bear once the whole family can be together permanently.[25] María Isabel makes a rational decision, but her decision cannot be abstracted from her ties and commitments to her extended family, Enrique, and her daughter.

Despite their shortcomings, agency-dominant understandings of migration make an appearance in many philosophical migration ethics. John Rawls, for example, considers immigration to be a problem that would disappear in an ideal world made up of decent or liberal peoples. His reasoning is that, since the push factors of migration, including poverty, war, and unemployment, would not exist in an ideal world, then neither would migration.[26] Other philosophical ethicists of migration follow Rawls's reasoning, assuming that wealthy countries are "besieged" by migrants from less-developed countries.[27]

Agency-dominant understandings of migration also inform public discussions of immigration. Neoclassical migration theory and its rational-agent anthropology lurk behind ethical perspectives that minimize the exploitation and abuse of migrants. By overemphasizing autonomy and rational choice, these theories can leave us with the impression that migrants cannot really be oppressed or exploited in their new countries.[28] They do, after all, have the freedom to return to their own countries should life in the new country become unbearable. Neoclassical migration theorist George Borjas writes the following concerning the exploitation of undocumented migrants in the United States:

> [T]hese persons are in the United States voluntarily. They willingly entered the black market for immigrants, and they obviously benefit from being in the United States, for otherwise, they would simply return to their country of origin where they could avoid the exploitation and stigma attached to illegal status.[29]

Borjas's unstated premise here, that migrants are fully informed rational agents, hampers his moral vision. The abuse and exploitation of undocu-

25. Nazario, *Enrique's Journey*, 237–40.

26. John Rawls, *The Law of Peoples* (Cambridge, MA: Harvard University Press, 1999), 8–9.

27. Walzer, *Spheres of Justice*, 40.

28. Tisha M. Rajendra, "The Rational Agent or the Relational Agent: Moving from Freedom to Justice in Migration Systems Ethics," *Ethical Theory and Moral Practice* 18 (2015): 355–69.

29. Borjas, *Friends or Strangers*, 72.

mented workers in industrialized countries are well-documented. Millions of undocumented workers labor without the protections of minimum wage, occupational safety, or the social welfare provisions that are afforded to citizens. Often, conditions for undocumented workers are little better than slavery.[30] But agency-dominant theories of migration leave Borjas without any way to understand the exploitation of migrant workers. If migrants choose to participate in an unjust system, even if it is for the benefit of their families and communities back home, then—so this reasoning goes—it cannot possibly be true exploitation.

That reasoning is echoed in policy discussions of immigration in which the choices of undocumented migrants are examined in a moral light.[31] Surely, if migrants choose to break the law, they should not be afforded its protection. Proposals arguing that undocumented migrants should have to go to the "back of the line" so as not to reward their unlawful behavior reflect this moralization of migrants' choice to migrate. On the flip side, migrants who come through lawful channels are often thought to be the "good" migrants, those who followed all the rules, at least as long as they follow the laws of their host country. If they do not, they are summarily deported, at which time the migrants' "choice" to break laws is again invoked, with little attention to the structural dimensions of the legal system that allows migrant lawbreakers to be deported without due process.[32]

The shortcomings of both the neoclassical view and the new economics of migration view were noted early on by migration theorists from the fields of sociology, anthropology, and demography. The search for a more comprehensive migration theory led to structure-dominant theories of migration that take the social nature of the person more seriously.

Structure-Dominant Theories of Migration

Rather than reducing migration to the aggregate of individual decisions, structure-dominant migration theories understand migration to be the result of economic, social, political, and historical structures that create the

30. Barry Estabrook, *Tomatoland: How Modern Industrial Agriculture Destroyed Our Most Alluring Fruit* (Kansas City, MO: Andrews McMeel Publishing, 2011), 73–74.

31. Heyer, *Kinship across Borders*, 139.

32. For an account of deportation in the United States, see Dan Kanstroom, *Deportation Nation: Outsiders in American History* (Cambridge, MA: Harvard University Press, 2007).

necessary conditions for migration.[33] Structure-dominant theories draw on Karl Marx's insight that market economies are driven by much more than the rational choices of self-interested actors. Marx and his intellectual heirs contend that national and global markets are built on the systemic exploitation of workers, especially those in developing nations, an exploitation that is made possible and perpetuated by unjust structures. Structural theorists of migration have used these insights to develop migration theories that emphasize the role of structures—that is, those political, economic, and social institutions that aggregate and extend the actions of a person beyond the time and space limits of those actions.

There are three major types of structure-dominant theories of migration: segmented-labor-market theory, historical-structural theory, and world-systems theory. Segmented-labor-market theory focuses on the labor markets of developed countries. This theory is rooted in Marx's insight that low-wage, low-skill, low-prestige jobs are a byproduct of industrialized economies.[34] The labor markets of industrialized countries are thus divided into two segments: a primary labor market of high-status, well-paid jobs and a secondary labor market of low-wage, low-prestige jobs. Though Marx was describing agricultural labor that required workers who could be hired and fired seasonally, segmented-labor-market theory develops this insight and applies it to the contemporary transnational labor market, which includes service and construction jobs in addition to agriculture.[35] The labor market is divided, not into two sectors, but into many. And the segments that are most dangerous, have the lowest status, and pay the least are often those where immigrants are to be found. Segmented-labor-market theorists would examine the story of Enrique's family and note that Lourdes migrated in response to the market demand for cheap labor in the United States. Furthermore, the jobs that Lourdes got once she arrived in the United States—domestic childcare and factory work—paid subminimum wage and offered no benefits.

The segmentation of the labor market is driven not only by the economic structures of the labor market but by the political and social structures of the country and the world. The division of the world into sovereign nation-states grants citizenship to some and denies it to others (Bauder, 26). Those without citizenship are perfectly positioned for the various segments

33. Goss and Lindquist, "Conceptualizing International Labor Migration," 322.

34. Harald Bauder, *Labor Movement: How Migration Regulates Labor Markets* (Oxford: Oxford University Press, 2005), 20. Hereafter, page references to this work appear in parentheses within the text.

35. Massey et al., *Worlds in Motion*, 30–31.

of the secondary labor market because they are the ultimate disposable labor force. Because she is not a citizen, Lourdes is unable to claim most of the protections the United States extends to its own citizens, such as unemployment benefits or minimum-wage protections (26). Lourdes's undocumented status and lack of education effectively shut her out of any but the bottom tier of the labor market (29–33). In addition, like many migrants, Lourdes faces a racist social discourse in the host country in which many citizens believe that migrants, by virtue of their culture and ethnicity, are better suited to the lower segments of the labor market (29).

While segmented-labor-market theory focuses on the labor markets of industrialized countries, historical-structural and world-systems theories view migration in the context of international economies, specifically the global transfer of resources from the developing world to the industrialized world. Historical-structural theory has its roots in Marxist dependency theory, in which migration, a legacy of colonial exploitation, becomes another way in which the resources of the developing world are transferred to the developed world.[36] In addition to mining the developing world for raw materials such as bananas and cobalt, now industrialized countries mine the developing world for cheap labor. World-systems theory, on the other hand, focuses on the role of multinational corporations in bringing about the conditions for migration in rural areas of the developing world by disrupting local economies, driving people into poverty, and displacing workers.[37]

Both historical-structural and world-systems theory focus, then, on the international structures that drive migration. These structures are larger than the economies of local communities and even national labor markets; they are historical and global in nature, rooted in geopolitical events that in some cases date back to the dawn of European colonization of the New World.

All three structure-dominant theories of migration reject the view of the person as an autonomous, rational agent; in fact, the *choice* to migrate plays hardly any role at all in these theories. This emphasis on the structures that drive international migration can helpfully counteract the dominant personal-agency narrative that seeks to punish undocumented migrants for breaking the law. Migrants are merely responding to the demands of the industrial economies in which they find themselves. It makes little sense to

36. For a fuller account of dependency theory, see Vincent Ferraro, "Dependency Theory: An Introduction," in *The Development Economics Reader*, ed. Ferraro (New York: Routledge, 2008).

37. Castles and Miller, *The Age of Migration*, 26.

build walls and reinforce borders (as Donald Trump has proposed) if the underlying structures remain intact.

Although structure-dominant theories of migration add to our understanding of migration, they are also inadequate since they neglect the importance of individual human agency. These theories risk viewing migrants as mere victims of these international structures. Enrique and his family have their own hopes, dreams, and stories, but their voices are not heeded in structure-dominant theories of migration. Migrants do choose to cross borders; many make difficult sacrifices in order to have money for remittances for their families who remain in their countries of origin. Many migrants start businesses, provide jobs for family members, and make friends and neighbors in the host countries. Surely, migrants are much more than the pawns and victims of international structures of migration. But structural theories of migration have no way to incorporate the agency, voices, and experiences of migrants into theories of the determinants of migration.

Also missing from structural theories of migration is the agency of those who *hire* migrants and participate in the transnational labor market in other ways. These theories provide no way to evaluate what it means to cooperate and participate in these structures of injustice, because, according to such theories, the structures are outside humans' control. The system rewards those who suppress wages in order to keep profits high, making the exploitation of immigrants inevitable. Adopting an exclusively structure-dominant account of migration releases both migrants and citizens from the moral obligation of assessing their participation in such structures.

In erasing the agency of both migrants and citizens from an account of migration, structure-dominant migration theories risk erasing the responsibility that both migrants and citizens have in creating and perpetuating these unjust structures. These structures might preexist all the migrants and citizens alive today, but that does not mean we bear no responsibility for reforming and, in some cases, resisting unjust structures.[38] In fact, many Christian migration ethicists hold out examples of churches and other groups who have resisted the dehumanizing structures that drive migration. For example, both the Dolores Mission Parish and the Kino Border Initiative described by Kristin Heyer and Ilsup Ahn practice a "subversive hospitality" that resists the unjust social structures that drive migration.[39] Theologically speaking, to ignore the agency and focus on structures exclusively is to devalue both

38. Heyer, *Kinship across Borders*, chap. 2.
39. Heyer, *Kinship across Borders*, 49–54, 158; Ahn, *Religious Ethics and Migration*, 182.

the freedom of the human individual and our responsibility for reforming or resisting unjust structures.

Migration-Systems Theory

I have argued in this chapter that both agency-dominant and structure-dominant theories of migration fall short because both of them ignore vital dimensions of who humans are, and both lead to unsatisfactory ethics of migration. By contrast, *migration-systems* theory shows how both the agency of migrants and the structures of migration are crucial to understanding transnational migration. Like agency-dominant theories of migration, migration-systems theory declares that migrants like Lourdes and Enrique make decisions for themselves and their families. However, unlike agency-dominant theories, migration-systems theory posits that people make these decisions in the context of political, economic, and historical structures. For example, Enrique and María Isabel would not and could not have made the decision to migrate in the absence of the many Hondurans who had made the trip before them.

Unlike structure-dominant theories of migration, migration-systems theory posits that while some structures preexist migration decisions, other structures are shaped by actions of migrants. In other words, when Lourdes migrates, it affects the actions of the migrants who come after her, including Enrique, María Isabel, and their daughter. Agency and structures affect and condition one another. Recognizing the role of both is essential for understanding migration.

Not all migration theorists recognize migration-systems theory as a separate type of migration theory. Some migration theorists subsume it under world-systems theory;[40] others describe migration systems not as a separate theory but as "a series of generalizations that can help provide an order for the analysis of the complexity of the real situation."[41] Whether migration-systems theory is a separate migration theory or is just a tool for understanding migration is less relevant for ethicists and theologians than it is for migration theorists. Regardless, migration-systems theory describes migration in a way that pays attention to both the agency of migrants and the larger structures that drive migration. It has enormous potential to help

40. Massey et al., *Worlds in Motion*, 61.
41. Skeldon, *Migration and Development*, 31.

Christian ethicists understand migration in all of its complexity and to lay the foundation for a Christian ethics of migration that justly responds to the relationships between citizens and migrants.

Migration-systems theory posits that transnational migration is made up of discrete, overlapping "migration systems," the exchanges of large numbers of migrants between two or more countries.[42] Postcolonial northern African labor migration to France is one such migration system; labor migration between the Philippines and the Middle East is another. In other words, instead of making generalizations about migration, migration-systems theory analyzes each migration system as a discrete phenomenon. Any migration system is the result of the interactions of macrostructures, mesostructures, and the micro-level decisions of migrants, their families, and their communities.

While migration-systems theory can be used to explain any kind of intracountry or transnational migration, I focus here on large-scale economic migrations from the developing world to Western democracies. At the macro-level, migration systems are generally initiated by three kinds of actions of the sending country: (1) colonial (and quasi-colonial) programs; (2) government-sponsored labor recruitment; and (3) foreign investment. Colonial ties, such as those between France and Morocco, Great Britain and India, and the United States and the Philippines, initiated migration systems when the citizens of former colonies, fluent in the language of the colonial power, responded to labor shortages in the host country. Quasi-colonial ties, such as US interventions in Guatemala and El Salvador, also generated migration systems.[43]

Government-sponsored labor recruitments have also initiated migration systems. Although these so-called guest-worker programs, used at various times by Germany, Belgium, France, Switzerland, and the United States, were designed as temporary programs to respond to postwar labor shortages, in each case the guest-worker programs started migration flows that continued well after the programs had ceased.

Foreign investment has a less clear causal connection with migration. However, certain kinds of foreign investment—specifically, investment in factories that manufacture goods for sale in the developed world—can initi-

---

42. Mary M. Kritz and Hania Zlotnik, "Global Interactions: Migration Systems, Processes, and Policies," in *International Migration Systems: A Global Approach*, ed. Mary M. Kritz, Lin Lean Lim, and Hania Zlotnik (Oxford: Clarendon Press, Oxford University Press, 1992), 4.

43. Sassen, *Guests and Aliens*, 138.

ate migration systems or augment existing migration systems. Such factories often disrupt traditional labor structures and initiate internal migration in which people move from rural areas to urban ones. When these factories close, they leave in their wake a new group of unemployed workers who have already left home. These workers are more likely to cross borders.[44]

Although migration systems are most often initiated by host countries, once they are started, they cannot be terminated at the will of the host country. This is because migration systems are perpetuated through the meso-structures of migration: social networks, businesses, and family connections that migrants draw on to help them move and adapt to their new homes.[45] These mesostructures can themselves span borders, stretching from ethnic enclaves in the new countries to the cities, towns, and villages in the migrants' homelands. Mesostructures "lower the costs and risks of migration," thereby having an impact on the micro-level decisions of migrants and their familes.[46]

The micro-level of migration is made up of the decisions of individuals and families who migrate for a variety of reasons that often include, but are not limited to, the economic well-being of their families. In other words, agency-dominant migration theories are correct in that migrants and their families do make decisions and that these decisions are based in part on their self-interest and the desire to provide for their families; however, these decisions take place within the context of these macro- and mesostructures of migration. In other words, the very choice to migrate can be conditioned by the macro- and mesostructures.

Conversely, the individual decisions of migrants and their families have an impact on and change the structures of migration. According to Massey et al., "Each act of migration alters the social context within which subsequent migration decisions are made, typically in ways that make additional movement more likely."[47] We can see this reflected at the individual level in the story of Enrique and his family. Lourdes's migration affects Enrique's decision, which affects María Isabel's. But there are also mesostructures at work in their story. The migration of Enrique's family conditions the environment in which the family's neighbors and friends will make their own decisions

44. Saskia Sassen, *The Mobility of Labor and Capital: A Study in International Investment and Labor Flow* (Cambridge: Cambridge University Press, 1988).

45. Thomas Faist, *The Volume and Dynamics of International Migration and Transnational Social Spaces* (Oxford: Clarendon Press, 2000), chap. 4.

46. Massey et al., *Worlds in Motion*, 42–43.

47. Massey et al., *Worlds in Motion*, 45–46.

about migration. In aggregate, these decisions encourage the formation of other mesostructures, such as the networks of human smugglers who promise to get Enrique and others like him to the United States. Migration-systems theory is thus able to account for patterns of migration that agency-dominant theories cannot. Although poverty and inequality are linked to migration, they need to be activated in some way to start a migration flow.[48] While agency-dominant migration theories would predict that migration will ebb and flow with unemployment and poverty rates in host countries, migration-systems theory understands that the mesostructures make migration somewhat autonomous from these variations. Thus, Sassen says, migration systems can and do continue past the end of the interventions of the host country. Though migration systems, in the absence of further interventions, do eventually end, it is rarely at the will or the convenience of the host country.

Unlike agency-dominant theories of migration, migration-systems theory can account for why groups of migrants go to some countries and not others. People generally do not migrate en masse in the absence of a preexisting migration system. Unlike both agency-dominant and structure-dominant theories, migration-systems theory can account for why some people migrate while most others do not. For instance, people whose family members and neighbors have migrated are more likely to migrate themselves.

Migration-systems theory, like segmented-labor-market theory, shows how the appetites of industrial countries for cheap labor fuel migration. However, migration-systems theory shows that the labor markets of receiving countries drive migration in geographically specific ways. The government-organized labor recruitment initiates a migration system. Once the program ends, the migration system continues, not only through migrant networks, but also often via the labor recruitment strategies of private corporations.[49] In other words, it is not only the economic structures of global capitalism that drive migration; it is also the specific actions of labor recruiters in host countries who initiate migration systems.

Migration-systems theory differs from historical-structural and world-systems theory in that it provides specificity and nuance to the account of

---

48. Sassen, *Guests and Aliens*, 136.

49. Alejandro Portes and József Böröcz, "Contemporary Immigration: Theoretical Perspectives on Its Determinants and Modes of Incorporation," *International Migration Review* 23, no. 3 (Autumn 1989): 611.

the exploitation of the developing world. The long history of exploitation between colonizers and colonized has involved specific and bounded relationships of domination and exploitation. These relationships, once started, continue because of the continued participation of citizens and migrants in the systems that result.

Migration-systems theory improves on both agency-dominant and structure-dominant theories of migration by paying attention to the role of both autonomy and social structures in migration. Just as neoclassical migration theory is founded on the presumption that humans are rational, autonomous agents, migration-systems theory is also founded on certain presumptions about humans. In this case, the anthropological presumptions of migration-systems theory fit in quite well with some feminist critiques of both autonomy and relationality. Feminist ethicist Margaret Farley argues that these two obligating features of persons, autonomy and relationality, exist in relationship to one another. Farley's phrase "freedom in relationality" captures how our freedom is "a response to what we already are and to what has become possible for us in terms of where we are."[50] In other words, we make free decisions as autonomous actors, but these decisions always take place within the context of the relationships, both chosen and unchosen, in which we find ourselves.

Farley's description of persons explains how agency can intersect with structures in migration processes. It would be a mistake to view migrants as lacking in agency, dragged around by the historical forces that began long ago. Migrants are indeed rational agents. They do make decisions about maximizing outcomes for themselves and their families. Lourdes, Enrique, and María Isabel all describe how difficult it was to leave their loved ones and the familiarity of home; but the promise of a better life for their children lured them away. These conflicted feelings about migration are echoed in many first-person accounts of migration in which migration is experienced not as the inevitable outcome of global economic structures but as a tragic choice born out of desperation to provide for families.

The decision to migrate, however, is historically embedded. Farley writes that this embeddedness is part of what relationality means: "[Persons] are in biological, psychological, cultural history, and their history is in them like the rings of a tree."[51] To be connected to other people is to be connected to history. Thus, the decision to migrate is historically conditioned, though

50. Farley, "A Feminist Version of Respect for Persons," 196.
51. Farley, "A Feminist Version of Respect for Persons," 195.

not determined. Migrants make decisions within this historical context of relationships between political communities.

Migration: A Relational Reality

Enrique and his mother, Lourdes, both came to the United States at great personal peril. Each migration theory that I have presented in this chapter would interpret their stories differently. (1) Neoclassical migration theory would say that both Enrique and Lourdes evaluated the economic opportunities at home or abroad and decided to go where they could maximize their earnings—the United States. (2) The new economics of migration would explain the migration of mother and son by echoing their own reasoning about providing for their families through their better-paying jobs in the United States. (3) Structure-dominant theories would look to the demand for cheap labor and conclude that the migrations of Lourdes and Enrique were driven by this demand. (4) Migration-systems theory would consider the decisions of both Lourdes and Enrique and the context of those decisions.[52] A brief examination of their stories, in which we use the tools of migration-systems theory, will show how migration-systems theory illuminates specific aspects of their story that are ignored by the other theories but are the key to the central concerns of this book.

Unlike other Central American countries, Honduras was not torn apart by civil war in the 1980s, as El Salvador and Guatemala were. These countries experienced massive waves of emigration in response to civil war; but there was little international migration from Honduras during the same period. This changed after the Cold War ended in 1989, when neoliberal economic reforms that were common in the region similarly affected Honduras. Specifically, the growth of factory work in urban areas caused much internal migration: people from the rural countryside moved to the cities to find work. Some of these uprooted workers made their way to the United States. In 1998, Hurricane Mitch struck Honduras, damaging factories and devastating the banana industry. The massive unemployment that followed caused a surge in the number of Hondurans who fled to the United States.[53]

52. Daniel Reichman, "Honduras: The Perils of Remittance Dependence and Clandestine Migration," *Migration Information Source*, April 11, 2013.
53. Reichman, "Honduras."

Lourdes left Honduras at the very beginning of the post-1989 wave of neoliberal reforms. In some ways she was a trailblazer, one of the first Hondurans to go to the United States seeking work. By the time Enrique decided to follow her (in 2001), the mesostructures of migration were firmly in place to transport undocumented Honduran migrants to the United States. Unlike Lourdes, who rode buses through Mexico with her smuggler, Enrique had to ride the tops of trains with hundreds of other migrants. When Enrique's girlfriend, María Isabel, set out to join him several years later, she made her decision in the context of the macrostructures of neoliberal economic reforms. The garment factories in Tegucigalpa hired only women who were between the ages of eighteen and twenty-five. Once a woman would reach her late twenties, her earning potential dropped sharply. With poverty and possibly unemployment looming, María Isabel left her daughter in the care of members of her family and set off to join Enrique. Lourdes thus set in motion an entire chain of migration within her own family: it eventually led to Enrique, María Isabel, and their daughter all relocating to the United States. As migration-systems theory would express it, each migration decision leads to the next, but they are all distinct. All the decisions took place within the context of the macro- and mesostructures that drive migration.

These migration decisions cannot be reduced to rational self-interest; neither should the voices and experiences of Lourdes and her family be reduced to the inevitable result of structures beyond their control. In this way, migration-systems theory highlights the fact that migration is the result of both historical and current relationships between and among migrants and citizens. At the same time, it highlights the fact that migrants have agency that is conditioned by and conditions these larger structures.

While agency-dominant migration theories present migration as the result of an aggregation of choices, and structure-dominant migration theories present migration as the inevitable result of transnational economic and political structures, migration-systems theory presents migration as a relational reality, the result of relationships both between sending and receiving countries and among migrants themselves. This understanding of migration as a relational reality changes the ethical questions raised by migration.

If we adopt the neoclassical understanding of migration as the result of an aggregation of individual choices to maximize utility by migrating, then a central ethical question could be: How do we respond to the vexing situation of migrants like Enrique? A logical response would be to argue that, though Enrique and his family are neither neighbors nor fellow US citizens of ours, they are persons who should not be in the position of having to choose between parenting their children and providing for them. If we adopt a structure-dominant understanding of migration, a central question might be: How should Christians understand their agency in response to the structures of migration? A logical answer might be that Christians have the responsibility to resist the unjust structures that drive migration. In presenting migration-systems theory, I do not wish to suggest either that advocating for migrants or that resisting unjust structures is inappropriate or un-Christian. On the contrary, these initiatives embody the corporeal works of mercy and witness to the humanity of migrants before a public discourse that often demonizes and scapegoats them.

I do wish to suggest, however, that the *relationships* between citizens and migrants that initiated and sustain migration systems must be at the heart of the Christian ethics of migration. Indeed, the central question of this book is: "What responsibilities do citizens have to migrants?" Responding to that question involves accurately understanding the relationships between different groups of citizens and migrants. In reviewing different migration theories, my aim has been to show that our understanding of migration drives our ethical questions and responses. Migration-systems theory has shown that migration is not, to return to Sassen's words, "an exogenous process, one formed and shaped by conditions outside the receiving country."[54] Receiving countries are not, in fact, "passive bystanders" to migration. Host countries have participated in migration systems.

But how, then, do we understand this participation? What is the ethical relevance of these kinds of relationships between migrants and citizens? In the following chapter I draw on migration-systems theory to offer new narratives that "retell" the story of relationships between migrants and citizens. Understanding the relationships between migrants and citizens as relationships of domination and exploitation that in some cases originated decades—or even centuries—ago will go a long way toward constructing an ethics of migration that not only invokes the human rights of migrants, but also specifies who has the duty to protect the rights of migrants and why.

For Further Reading

Migration theory is a vast and diverse field. A quick introduction geared toward lay readers is Stephen Castles and Mark Miller's *The Age of Migration*

54. Sassen, *Guests and Aliens*, 136.

(New York: Guilford, 2009), which is updated in a new edition every four years or so. Another helpful resource is Douglas S. Massey et al., *Worlds in Motion* (Oxford: Oxford University Press, 2005).

This chapter draws extensively on the insights of migration theorist Saskia Sassen. A succinct introduction to her work and its ethical implications is found in her essay entitled "The Making of Migrations," a chapter in *Living with(out) Borders: Catholic Theological Ethics on the Migration of Peoples*, edited by Agnes M. Brazal and María T. Dávila (Maryknoll, NY: Orbis, 2016).

CHAPTER 3

In Search of Better Narratives

Every ethics of migration, every immigration policy proposal, and every public discourse about migrants implicitly draw on narratives about migrants: who they are, why they left home, and why they came to their new country. As we have seen, many of these narratives are false to some degree. Some of these narratives are racist on their face, such as the narratives that portray migrants as freeloaders who come to sponge off a welfare state. Other narratives are well-meaning but still inaccurate, such as those that portray migrants as the poorest and most vulnerable people. Inaccurate narratives lead us to ask the wrong questions; at other times they can lead us to become satisfied with the wrong answers. Narratives have the potential to either obscure moral realities or to illuminate them. In order to recognize narratives as false, however, we must scrutinize them using the tools of migration theory, sociology, theology, and history. We can then seek to replace the inaccurate narratives with fuller narratives that are more "faithful to reality."[1]

Sorting through what kinds of relationships yield what kinds of responsibilities is no easy task. Philosopher Margaret Urban Walker argues that three kinds of narratives are critical for sorting through responsibilities: narratives of relationship, identity, and value.[2] These three narratives intertwine to make it possible to live a moral life. If relationships are the grounds of responsibilities, narratives of relationship help us "acknowledge the past character, present state, and future possibilities of that relationship."[3] With-

---

1. This is a slight rewording of Jon Sobrino's phrase "honest towards reality" (Sobrino, *Where Is God? Earthquake, Terrorism, Barbarity, and Hope* [Maryknoll, NY: Orbis, 2004], chap. 2).

2. Margaret Urban Walker, *Moral Understandings: A Feminist Study in Ethics* (New York: Routledge, 1998), 117.

3. Walker, *Moral Understandings*, 117.

out a history of the relationship, an analysis of its present state, and a deter-
mination of whether and how the relationship might change in the future,
it is impossible to determine what responsibilities might arise from that relationship. A narrative helps make sense of the relationship. What Walker
calls "cases of purely episodic dependency," in which the other is a stranger
in desperate need, are straightforward but rare.[4]

In this chapter I retell the stories of the relationships between specific
migrants and citizens in order to examine the histories, present conditions, and possible futures of these relationships. I have chosen examples
from each of the three kinds of foreign interventions that initiate migration systems: guest-worker programs, colonialism, and foreign investment. The guest-worker program section draws heavily on the history
of the German program, though I do draw on the experience of other
countries in order to point to some structural features of these programs.
The colonialism section focuses primarily on the relationship between the
citizens of Great Britain and their former colonial subjects. The foreign
investment section focuses on the relationship between the United States
and Mexico.

The narratives presented here are not meant to be comprehensive histories; rather, I intend them to point out some structural features of these
kinds of interventions that are relevant for our understanding of the relationships between migrants and citizens that result. Rather than attempt to
provide complete narratives, I have strived to capture the ethically relevant
heart of the narratives that can illuminate the responsibilities of citizens to
migrants. These narratives are meant to offer a new way of thinking about the
relationships between migrants and citizens. Like all storytellers, I have had
to make decisions about what to include and what to leave out, what to emphasize and what to de-emphasize. Others may think I have left out critical
information or made too much of a minor point. But these narratives are not
meant to be the final word on relationships between citizens and migrants.
They can—and should—be expanded, revised, and critiqued.

Structural Sin as Relational Sin

Before proceeding to the retelling of the narratives of relationships between
migrants and citizens, I wish to bring the concept of structural sin or in-

---

4. Walker, *Moral Understandings*, 117.

justice to this examination of narratives.[5] Narratives can be more or less faithful to reality. When inaccurate narratives that are divorced from reality become the dominant social understanding of a group of people, something more insidious than divergent or competing narratives is at play. Liberation theologians would call this structural sin, that is, sin that appears not in the human will alone but in social institutions, ideologies, and practices.[6] Structural sin affects narratives of relationships in two ways: (1) it entrenches inaccurate narratives, and (2) it conditions relationships into patterns of domination and exploitation.

Theologians have long pointed out how structural sin appears in ideologies that "distort reality" and "legitimate unjust institutions."[7] Kristin Heyer cites as an example of these ideologies the media portrayal of immigrants as freeloaders, as well as a consumerist ideology that "shapes citizens' willingness to underpay or mistreat undocumented persons."[8] But ideologies do not simply appear as freestanding ideas. They undergird such inaccurate narratives of relationships between citizens and migrants. Media portrayals of immigrants as freeloaders are not so much an ideology as a series of stories about how and why immigrants came to the host country—and what they are doing now. Underlying this narrative is an ideology of the racial inferiority of Latinos as lazy and irresponsible. Similarly, consumer willingness to mistreat undocumented workers results from a narrative like that of Borjas (discussed in the preceding chapter): these workers are here voluntarily, participating in the free market; if they don't like the wages or the working conditions, they can get another job or go home. Inaccurate narratives are often premised on the ideologies that make up unjust social structures. Because these narratives are thus structurally entrenched and shape how we understand our social world, they often seem so obvious to us that they escape scrutiny.

The second way that narratives intersect with structural sin is that structural sin often conditions both our relationships with one another and the

---

5. Theologians use the term "sin," and philosophers use the term "injustice"; for my purposes, I use these terms interchangeably.

6. For a thorough account of social sin, see Kristin E. Heyer, "Social Sin and Immigration: Good Fences Make Bad Neighbors," *Theological Studies* 71 (2010): 410–36. For a philosophical account of structural injustice, see Iris Marion Young, *Responsibility for Justice* (Oxford: Oxford University Press, 2011), chap. 2. Hereafter, page references to Young's work appear in parentheses within the text.

7. Heyer, *Kinship across Borders*, 46.

8. Heyer, *Kinship across Borders*, 47.

narratives that we have about these relationships. In her book *Responsibility for Justice* (posthumously published in 2011), political philosopher Iris Marion Young examines the way that our agency can be constrained by social structures. These social structures, when functioning well, can enable us to flourish. However, they can also "put large groups of people under systematic threat of domination or deprivation of the means to develop and exercise their capacities" (52). Both Heyer and Ilsup Ahn have argued that the social structures driving migration are not morally neutral; rather, they are unjust, or even sinful.[9] In addition to shaping and conditioning the very choice to migrate, these social structures shape and condition the relationships between migrants and citizens.

One way that Young presents these social structures is as a "macro social space in which positions are related to one another" (53). In other words, persons are situated in social positions that define "whether they are socially 'close' or 'distant,' whether they are liable to identify with one another or express a sense of otherness" (56). In other words, when we relate to other persons in society, we are not just relating to them as complete free persons. Our relationships are in some sense conditioned by our relative social positions. "Sociologically, these relations position people prior to their interaction, and condition expectations and possibilities of interaction" (57). For example, when Lourdes is employed as a nanny, the relationship between her and the couple employing her is not only a relationship among three individuals. The relationship between these individuals is shaped by the numerous relationships of social position between undocumented domestic workers and upper-middle-class, double-income suburbanites, between Latinas and whites, and between citizens and migrants. In other words, the fact that Lourdes's wages fall far below a living wage is not simply the result of her employers not paying her enough: the interaction between Lourdes and her employers is, to a certain extent, conditioned by the relationship between undocumented migrants and citizens in Los Angeles. It is characteristic of the relationship between these two groups that citizens tend to underpay migrants, taking advantage of the cheap labor that they offer.

This understanding of the social position between citizens and migrants in the domestic sphere can be expanded to the relationships that drive transnational migration. Migration-systems theory illustrates how the social-structural processes that govern migration include not only global

---

9. Ahn, *Religious Ethics and Migration*, chap. 2; Heyer, *Kinship across Borders*, chap. 2.

economic structures and transnational labor markets but the entire field of social positions that was established decades ago by the actions of host countries. Elsewhere, Young writes that social structures are "recursive": that is, when people act, they act in conformity to unspoken and unwritten social rules.[10] Heyer describes a similar phenomenon when she points out that the nature of social sin is both "consequential and causal."[11] Once the structures of sin are in place, they distort our consciences, creating a malformation of our perceptions of right and wrong. They determine what we are able to see—or perhaps, more accurately, what we are conditioned to pay attention to.[12] They condition the options we see for ourselves in terms of our own actions. The same social structural processes that have positioned migrants and citizens in relationship to one another are in part responsible for the fact that citizens are in many cases able to remain ignorant of their relationships to migrants, enabling the reproduction of these relationships over generations.

In other words, the narrative of relationships past and present must not only consider histories of events, choices, and actions, but must also incorporate this way of thinking about social position. Without these structural considerations, we risk losing the continuity between past, present, and future in which social positions established in the past in some ways condition our relationships in the present and the future.

Narratives of Relationships Past

Guest-Worker Programs

Many of the largest migrations to Western Europe and the United States were initiated by guest-worker programs, in which Western governments responded to labor shortages by recruiting workers in other countries for temporary stays. Although the particulars of the guest-worker programs vary quite a bit from one country to another, all of these programs share some core similarities. In each program, the governments of host countries

10. Iris Marion Young, *Justice and the Politics of Difference* (Princeton: Princeton University Press, 1990), 60.

11. Heyer, "Social Sin and Immigration," 425.

12. Kenneth R. Himes, "Human Failing: The Meanings and Metaphors of Sin," in *Moral Theology: New Directions and Fundamental Issues*, ed. James Keating (New York: Paulist Press, 2004).

deliberately recruited foreign laborers in cooperation with foreign governments to address temporary labor shortages. Even though the intention was for the workers to return home within a few years, in every case the guest-worker programs led to permanent migration. This mismatch between the intention of the host countries and the results of their actions was possible because these programs were premised on relationships in which citizens commodified the guest workers.

Guest-worker programs were thought to be a good deal for host countries only because they were based on the fact that guest workers were not citizens. Therefore, host countries assumed that guest workers would either leave of their own accord, or they could be deported to their home countries after their work assignments ended.[13] German sociologist Christian Joppke writes that this assumption of return migration is "the very rationale of a guest worker regime, which sees foreign labour as a conjuncturally disposable commodity without social reproduction and education costs."[14]

Host countries thought these workers could subsidize the social welfare system without putting any burdens on it. Young, healthy, and single, they were unlikely to fall ill and burden a health system, or start families whose children would need education and health care.[15] Accordingly, these guest workers did necessary labor in the host countries but were provided with few of the benefits that citizens had secured for themselves. Citizens thought that they need not make the same kinds of social, economic, or educational investments in the guest workers that they made in their fellow citizens.

Another advantage of guest-worker programs is that guest workers accepted lower wages and lower labor standards than native workers, and they had little political voice with which to advocate for themselves. For example, guest workers in Germany were thought to be "more willing than Germans to accept unpleasant tasks and jobs, put in overtime hours, and tolerate a low standard of living because they intended to return home as soon as they had earned enough money" (Chin, 41). Guest workers not only

13. Christian Joppke, *Immigration and the Nation-State: The United States, Germany, and Great Britain* (Oxford: Oxford University Press, 1999), chap. 3; see also Rita C.-K. Chin, *The Guest Worker Question in Postwar Germany* (Cambridge: Cambridge University Press, 2007), 48.

14. Joppke, *Immigration and the Nation-State*, 65.

15. Chin, *The Guest Worker Question in Postwar Germany*, 45. Hereafter, page references to this work appear in parentheses within the text. See also Cindy Hahamovitch, *No Man's Land: Jamaican Guestworkers in America and the Global History of Deportable Labor* (Princeton: Princeton University Press, 2011), 8.

did the least appealing and worst-paying jobs; they also lacked the political power to pursue change in their situations. In the United States, this lack of political power was used to break the power of unions. Unlike unionized employees, guest workers could not protest their treatment or strike without consequences. If they did, they would simply be deported.[16] Guest workers all over Europe and the United States had few political rights and little say about the conditions they lived and worked in. Of guest workers, Michael Walzer writes: "These guests experience the state as a pervasive and frightening power that shapes their lives and regulates their every move—and never asks for their opinion."[17]

In other words, guest-worker programs were premised on the very differences in standing between citizens and guest workers. While fellow citizens were considered embodied persons with a full range of human relationships, the guest workers were only laborers. Citizens would age, fall sick, and have children; but guest workers could be returned to their home countries once they or their families required provisions for old age or disability from citizens. While citizens were members of the political community with full standing to advocate for themselves, guest workers were "disposable commodities." Guest-worker programs are founded on a dehumanization of labor itself, in which people could be used for their labor but be separated from the political community (Chin, 48). To quote Michael Walzer again: "Without the denial of political rights and civil liberties and the ever-present threat of deportation, the system would not work."[18]

Though guest-worker programs were initiated by host countries with the expectation that the guest workers would return to their home countries, they instead initiated migration systems that are in place to this day. In her magisterial study of mass migrations in Europe, Saskia Sassen says that guest-worker programs have always led to permanent settlements.[19] Thus, though the programs discussed in this chapter had mostly ended by the 1960s and 1970s, the programs resulted in migrant populations that now form permanent ethnic minorities in many Western countries.[20]

16. Hahamovitch, *No Man's Land*, 234.

17. Walzer, *Spheres of Justice*, 59.

18. Walzer, *Spheres of Justice*, 59.

19. Sassen, *Guests and Aliens*, 143.

20. Hahamovitch points out that, though the United States *bracero* program formally ended in 1964, the United States still relies on guest workers through the H2–A and B visa program (Hahamovitch, *No Man's Land*, 234).

How do temporary guest-worker programs lead to permanent migration? It turns out that humans cannot be reduced to their labor without the laborers claiming their full humanity. In the oft-quoted words of Swiss writer Max Frisch: "We wanted workers. We got people instead." In Germany, the guest-worker program was originally intended to rotate workers so that, as one set of visas expired, they would be replaced by new workers from the sending country. However, soon after the beginning of the program, employers discovered that it was more efficient to retain the workers they already had on renewable visas rather than pay the costs of training new workers on a regular basis (Chin, 49). "Temporary" guest workers thus spent decades working in Germany. The workers who arrived when they were young and single would not remain so. In 1972, Turkish and Yugoslav guest workers petitioned the German courts for the right of family reunification—and won.[21] Once the German courts awarded guest workers the right to bring their families to Germany on family reunification visas, the population of migrants continued to grow, even though the German guest-worker program was suspended in 1973. The guest workers were human beings with family ties who made decisions within the context of the larger macro- and mesostructures of guest-worker programs, family reunification policies, and their own social networks.

In addition to creating permanent ethnic minorities, guest-worker programs are thought to lead to a simultaneous increase in the population of undocumented migrants in the host country. Guest-worker programs are correlated with rises in the numbers of unauthorized border crossings. In addition, guest workers often become undocumented as soon as they walk off an abusive job. Although guest-worker programs are often proposed as a solution to undocumented migration, as historian Cindy Hahamovitch puts it, these "two systems of recruiting foreign labor have always existed in symbiosis."[22] Migration theorists have made a similar point in noting that government-sponsored, temporary labor-migration programs often operate concurrently with private corporate recruitment in ways that tacitly encourage undocumented migration.[23] Undocumented migrants are often exploited in the same kinds of ways that guest workers are. They are paid lower wages, without benefits or access to a social safety net, and they have

21. Joppke, *Immigration and the Nation-State*, 74–75.

22. Hahamovitch, *No Man's Land*, 237.

23. Alejandro Portes and József Böröcz, "Contemporary Immigration: Theoretical Perspectives on Its Determinants and Modes of Incorporation," *International Migration Review* 23, no. 3 (1989): 606–30.

been used to break the power of unions. Even though the guest-worker programs described here ended decades ago, the relationship between citizens and migrants that developed in the instantiation and the execution of these programs continues in a different form today as undocumented workers, often of the same ethnicity as the original guest workers, fulfill citizens' needs for a disposable labor force.

Until 1992, Germany's laws denied citizenship—and thus full membership in German society—to even the children and grandchildren of guest workers. Even then, the citizenship laws of that country did not change to accommodate immigrants and their children until 2000. Rita Chin argues that these reforms would not have been possible without "the agency of the migrants themselves and their decades-long efforts to claim a space within the national body" (264). Hence, while political oppression and exclusion form a key part of the narrative of the relationship, for example, between German citizens and their guest workers, another part of the narrative of this relationship is how the guest workers claimed for themselves a space in German society. And this narrative of the past relationship continues today.

Thus, in many European countries, the narrative of the relationship between citizens and migrants begins not with the terrorist attacks of the twenty-first century, nor with the problems of multiculturalism that emerged in the late twentieth century, but with the instantiation of these postwar guest-worker programs. Today, guest workers and their descendants make up the largest portion of Germany's nearly eight million immigrants.[24] In Germany, the descendants of guest workers remain clustered in low-wage labor; their education levels are lower than those of the general population; and they often face discrimination in the labor and housing markets.[25] However, they are, by virtue of their citizenship, their language, and the land of their birth, indisputably German.

The narratives of relationships past and present have implications for the identities of both parties. Chin argues that contemporary debates about multiculturalism, the role of Islam, and what it means to be German (or, by implication, Belgian or Swiss) cannot be separated from these narratives of relationships past. Like reunification, labor migration, Chin argues, was a "foundational event in the constitution of the modern German nation" (272).

24. Veysel Oezcan, "Germany: Immigration in Transition," Migration Information Source, July 1, 2004, http://www.migrationinformation.org/feature/display.cfm?ID=235.

25. Matthias Bartsch, Andrea Brandt, and Daniel Steinvorth, "Turkish Immigration to Germany: A Sorry History of Self-Deception and Wasted Opportunities," *Spiegel Online*, September 7, 2010.

Guest workers were "less a footnote to [Germany's postwar] economic miracle than one of its sustaining forces" (265). Though no one intended for guest workers and their descendants to become a part of Europe, they are now.

Colonial Migration Systems

Like guest-worker programs, colonial foreign policies resulted in some of the largest migrations from the developing world to the developed world. Although Western colonialism dates back to the first ships that left Europe in search of the New World, I will here examine only colonial relationships that generated the migration flows that dominate political discourse in the United States and Western Europe today, with a particular focus on Great Britain.

While it is difficult to make generalizations about a system of governance that spans so many centuries and histories, colonialism is at heart "a form of domination which involves the subjugation of one people by another." This domination usually involves the "denial of self-determination and the imposition of rules from a separate political jurisdiction." In addition to political domination, colonialism has historically often included an element of cultural domination as well, in which the colonial power attempts to "impose [its] culture and customs onto the colonized." Daniel Butt notes that, though different intentions and motivations drove colonial powers, exploitation has always been a key part of colonialism. Various slave trades, the appropriation of natural and cultural resources, and exploitative trade relations are all linked to colonialism.[26]

Political scientist Catherine Lu highlights the structural dimension of colonial injustices. Unlike war crimes, for which wrongdoers can be and historically have been held accountable, colonial injustices "[do] not fit into a typical way of thinking about the nature and circumstances of wrongdoing, as an aberrant and willful violation of shared communal norms, laws, or practices."[27] Colonial policies were once legal according to international law, and in pursuing colonial policies, states were conforming to, rather than deviating from, "shared communal norms, laws, and practices." Even though colonial

---

26. Daniel Butt, "Colonialism and Postcolonialism," in *The International Encyclopedia of Ethics*, ed. Hugh LaFollette (Oxford: Wiley-Blackwell, 2013), 892–98.

27. Catherine Lu, "Colonialism as Structural Injustice: Historical Responsibility and Contemporary Redress," *Journal of Political Philosophy* 19, no. 3 (2011): 266.

policies were legal at the time, such policies were premised on their own ideologically driven narratives about colonized peoples—namely, colonized peoples were not ready for self-governance. They were racially and intellectually inferior to the colonizers and could only benefit from foreign governance. Their own languages, cultures, and civilizations were vastly inferior to those of Europe, and they would gain from instruction—even if it was coerced.[28]

While the narrative of the history of guest-worker programs tends to be ignored or forgotten, the narratives of colonial pasts are often not forgotten, but glorified. A 2005 law passed by the French National Assembly required schools to teach about the positive aspects of colonialism. Though this law was repealed a mere eight months after it passed, the fact that it was proposed at all suggests that in France the colonial narrative has yet to be fully reckoned with. Similarly, in Great Britain, the statues of colonial administrators grace public spaces, commemorating the achievements of these men while obscuring their participation in colonial programs.

One could argue in defense of the public commendations of these men that, until the 1960 plenary meeting of the United Nations General Assembly, colonialism was not a violation of international law. One could also argue that the racist ideologies that drove the narratives about the justness of colonial programs were thought, at the time, to be merely the facts of biology. In order to reflect on the distinction between structural injustice (in which people are acting according to unjust shared moral norms) and individual and corporate wrongdoing (in which people and states commit wrongdoing), Lu proposes that we try to see colonialism as an expression of structural injustice rather than individual or corporate wrongdoing, so we can better understand how to justly respond to the past.

Lu's proposal can have an impact on the narratives about a colonial past. The dismissal of colonialism as the product of a racist past and the condemning of the long-dead colonizers as evil both sever the unity of the narrative of past, present, and future. Lu's proposal, on the other hand, suggests that we can incorporate this narrative of structurally unjust relationships in order to understand both the moral culpability of those in the past and how those past relationships form present-day relationships between citizens and migrants.

British immigration was a direct consequence of British colonialism. Even though the British economy relied on the low-wage labor that migrants provided, the British governments never deliberately recruited foreign labor

28. Lu, "Colonialism as Structural Injustice," 267.

during the post–World War II period.[29] Thus, unlike Germany and France, Great Britain never had a guest-worker program. Instead, British immigration from former colonies in the twentieth century was a direct result of the fact that Great Britain's "political boundaries were wider than the nation."[30] With Great Britain colonizing as much as one-fifth of the earth's land mass, up to a quarter of the world's people were at one time British subjects. Because there was no legal distinction between a British subject and a British citizen, colonial subjects could move freely within the empire. Thus, when the first Jamaicans arrived on British shores in 1948, they had every legal right to be there.

While the British public was largely complicit with the colonial project, they were uncomfortable with its results. Although the public had no problem welcoming ethnically English descendants of the colonists after decolonization, they balked at the idea of living alongside black and brown people who were former colonial subjects. The racism on which the colonial project was founded was revealed as the British parliament scrambled to pass laws that would prevent the entrance of immigrants of color. In the 1970s, the British parliament ended family reunification visas, which ripped families apart.[31] In 1981, parliament passed the British Nationality Act, which demoted colonial subjects of color to a kind of citizenship that conferred no right of entry into or residence in the territory.

The British immigration story mirrors, to a certain extent, the history of migration to other former colonial powers. France also extended citizenship to people in its colonies. As in the British history, the migration flow to France was initiated by the fact that the colonial power had granted citizenship to colonial subjects, who were then not only equipped with fluency in the language and familiarity with the customs of the colonial power, but with the citizenship of that country. However, in postwar France the colonial migration flow was augmented by postwar labor recruitment programs that encouraged colonial citizens to migrate in order to solve labor shortages.[32] While British subjects were eventually stripped of the right of immigration, and while former French citizens lost their citizenship upon decolonization, migration in both countries continued through family reunification visas, just as it had in Germany after the termination of guest-

---

29. Castles and Miller, *The Age of Migration*, 20.

30. Joppke, *Immigration and the Nation-State*, 102.

31. Joppke, *Immigration and the Nation-State*, 116; chap. 4.

32. Martin Schain, *The Politics of Immigration in France, Britain, and the United States: A Comparative Study* (New York: Palgrave Macmillan, 2008), 48.

worker programs. In the parlance of migration-systems theory, once the migration system was initiated, the migrant networks of family continued the migration flow.

Like the guest-worker programs, which led to permanent residence in the host country, colonial programs unintentionally set in motion migrations that helped make the United Kingdom what it is today—a diverse, multicultural country with peoples who can trace their origins to regions all across the globe. Because of England's colonial past, German Cardinal Walter Kaspar could complain in 2010, "When you arrive in Heathrow airport, you think at times that you've landed in a Third World Country."[33]

Beginning the story of British or French migration with colonialism changes the narrative of the relationship between citizens and migrants in both countries. The ideology of racial inferiority translated itself into social relationships of domination and exploitation in which the colonizers subjugated the colonized. When these colonial migrations started, then continued past the independence of the decolonized country, the social relationships of domination and exploitation remained intact. These workers helped solve a labor shortage that the British government never acknowledged, yet they have remained in positions of occupational, social, and educational disadvantage for decades.[34] These migrants did not arrive only because they were poor and were seeking better economic opportunities. In words attributed to Stuart Hall, "They are here because we were there."

As in the case of Germany's guest-worker program, British colonialism and the subsequent migrations it engendered changed British society, which today is rife with reminders of colonialism, not only in the presence of these migrants and their descendants, but in British food and culture. In the words of novelist Zadie Smith, "There is no one more English than the Indian, no one more Indian than the English."[35] In other words, these relationships with colonial subjects changed what it means to be British. Yet the narrative of the past relationship between British citizens and these migrants is in some ways a story of relationships denied. The long history of restrictive immigration laws, the fiction that Britain is a country of "zero-immigration," and the emergence in the 1970s of racial slurs aimed at peoples of South Asian descent suggest that false narratives of the past lead to false narratives of the

33. Nick Squires and Martin Beckford, "Pope Visit: Cardinal Drops out after Calling UK 'Third World,'" *The Telegraph*, September 15, 2010, http://www.telegraph.co.uk/news/world news/the-pope/8004493/Pope-visit-Cardinal-drops-out-after-calling-UK-Third-World.html.

34. Castles and Miller, *The Age of Migration*, 102.

35. Zadie Smith, *White Teeth* (New York: Random House, 2000), 327.

present and future. Unlike Turkish migration to Germany, which has largely ended (more Turks returned to Turkey in 2013 than migrated from Turkey to Germany), immigration to the United Kingdom from many of its former colonies continues. In 2013 alone, a total of 53,000 migrants from India, Pakistan, and Malaysia immigrated to the United Kingdom. The migration flow continues.

Foreign Investment

The third kind of intervention that can lead to migration flows is foreign investment. Of the three kinds of interventions, foreign investment is the most complex, in part because foreign-investment relationships are so often layered on other kinds of historical relationships. In addition, foreign investment does not reliably lead to migration flows. As Saskia Sassen points out, the particular *kind* of investment matters a great deal.[36] For example, Café Justo, a coffee cooperative in the Mexican state of Chiapas, has provided jobs for farmers in its community, which has reduced the incentive to migrate.[37] However, other kinds of foreign investment have either initiated migration flows or intensified migration flows already in progress. Because of the complexities involved in making generalizations about foreign investment and migration, I will focus here on how foreign investment in export-oriented manufacturing has impacted the migration system between the United States and Mexico. Like guest-worker programs and colonialism, foreign investment in export-oriented factories is often itself the result of asymmetrical relationships between two countries.

The investment of US companies in Mexico takes place in the context of a preexisting migration system that dates back to the late nineteenth century, when US employers turned to Mexico as a source for foreign labor after immigration from China and Japan had been terminated (in the 1880s).[38] US labor recruitment in Mexico continued in one form or another until 1965, after which the social networks begun by the guest workers continued to

36. Sassen, *The Mobility of Labor and Capital*, 98.
37. Regan, *The Death of Josseline*, chap. 2.
38. Douglas S. Massey, Jorge Durand, and Nolan J. Malone, *Beyond Smoke and Mirrors: Mexican Immigration in an Era of Economic Integration* (New York: Russell Sage Foundation, 2002), 27.

bring migrants to the United States.[39] In other words, migration systems initiated by both private companies and government guest-worker programs had been in place for decades, and this history forms the context of US investment in Mexico.

Foreign investment in Mexico also takes place in the context of increasing economic integration between the two countries. Mexico's 1986 entry into the General Agreement on Tariffs and Trade (GATT) marked a shift in Mexican economic policy toward a neoliberal paradigm that encouraged production of Mexican goods for the international market.[40] This trajectory continued with the signing of the 1994 North American Free Trade Agreement (NAFTA). Studying the effects of economic integration on migration is an enormously complex task, in part because it is difficult to isolate the specific effect of economic integration from other confounding factors. For example, the signing of NAFTA was almost immediately followed by the Mexican peso crisis, which decimated the Mexican economy during a concurrent economic boom in the United States that resulted in historically low unemployment. While some scholars speculate that NAFTA caused the increase in undocumented migration that followed by aggravating economic inequalities between the two countries, others speculate that US intervention into the peso crisis might have helped stabilize the Mexican economy, preventing even higher rates of migration.[41] Despite the lack of scholarly consensus on the general effects of economic integration on migration, it is clear NAFTA did not curtail migration. Though many proponents of NAFTA predicted that it would reduce migration pressures by creating factory work in Mexico, the opposite happened. Increased migration may have been the result of the increase in factory work.

The idea that the creation of "export processing zones" increases migration is known as the "Sassen thesis,"[42] from Saskia Sassen's book *The Mobility of Labor and Capital* (1988), an examination of the relationship between this specific type of foreign investment and migration between the United States

39. Massey et al., *Beyond Smoke and Mirrors*, 42. Portes and Böröcz point out that labor recruitment in the developing world is still underway through private entities. Nowadays, the migrants themselves bear the costs of the journey (Portes and Böröcz, "Contemporary Immigration," 611).

40. Massey et al., *Beyond Smoke and Mirrors*, 78.

41. Demetrios G. Papademetriou, "The Shifting Expectations of Free Trade and Migration," in *NAFTA's Promise and Reality: Lessons from Mexico for the Hemisphere* (2004): 53.

42. Russell King and Ronald Skeldon, "Mind the Gap: Integrating Approaches to Internal and International Migration," *Journal of Ethnic and Migration Studies* 36, no. 10 (2010): 1624.

and Mexico. Though this book was published only two years after Mexico entered GATT and well before the ratification of NAFTA, Sassen's thesis is relevant to both treaties because both encouraged the creation of factories through the elimination of tariffs on imports. Raw materials can thus be imported to Mexico, turned into goods for sale, and exported without taxes. According to Sassen, the creation of these factories often disrupts traditional work structures by drawing people from traditional work in agriculture or crafts into work in factories.[43] Not only does the creation of factories draw people from traditional work, whose infrastructure collapses in the absence of workers, but the promise of factory work draws new people into the work force, particularly women.[44] Though these effects of the transition from an agricultural economy to a manufacturing one have long been a feature of industrialization,[45] in Mexico this process was exacerbated by the elimination of government grain subsidies to Mexico's farmers, which made it difficult for them to compete with an influx of cheap grain from the United States.[46]

The rural-urban migration within Mexico, accelerated by the *maquiladora* zones and the elimination of agricultural subsidies by the Mexican government, resulted in higher rates of migration to the United States. People who migrate within a country are far more likely to migrate internationally, in part because they have already been uprooted once.[47] Low-wage, strenuous labor in factories also has extremely high turnover. Rather than returning to traditional work, or leaving the work force altogether, newly unemployed workers were more likely to migrate to the United States where wages were much higher. This trend accelerated after the *maquiladoras* that had opened in the wake of NAFTA closed as manufacturers sought even cheaper labor in Asia.

Assessing the impact of free-trade policies as a whole is an enormous and complex task that is beyond the scope of this book. But we can draw a few ethical conclusions about NAFTA. Without a doubt, NAFTA has depressed wages in Mexico, increased income inequality, and ravaged the commercial agricultural industry there.[48] Regardless of the impact of economic integration as a whole, it is beyond dispute that NAFTA did not bring the

43. Sassen, *The Mobility of Labor and Capital*, 53.

44. Sassen, *The Mobility of Labor and Capital*, 116.

45. Papademetriou, "The Shifting Expectations," 46.

46. Sandra Polaski, "Jobs, Wages, and Household Income," in *NAFTA's Promise and Reality: Lessons from Mexico for the Hemisphere* (2004): 11–58.

47. King and Skeldon, "Mind the Gap," 1624.

48. Polaski, "Jobs, Wages, and Household Income."

promised benefits to Mexico's poor. But it did benefit US corporations a great deal.

Kristin Heyer argues that this very asymmetry of benefits indicates that the structures of economic integration are indeed structures of sin that dehumanize the labor of Mexico's factory workers.[49] Though economic integration was touted as a way to create jobs in Mexico, the jobs that were created were appalling in terms of working conditions, hours, and wages. Once labor markets opened in Asian countries—where the wages were even lower than in Mexico—many of the *maquiladoras* closed and relocated there, leaving workers far from home and without jobs. The global financial system is a sinful structure that rewards profit over the dignity of workers.[50] Rather than protecting either farmers or factory workers in Mexico, free-trade policies benefited both corporations and first-world consumers by maximizing profits while keeping the cost of goods low. Hence, as Ilsup Ahn points out, given the global economic structures and trade agreements that influence migration, US citizens are "unfair beneficiaries or even complacent accomplices of an unjust international economic system."[51] The global economic structures thus position US and Mexican citizens in relationships to one another that are structurally unjust.

Although foreign investment and economic integration form an important part of the narrative of the past relationship between migrants and citizens, these economic interventions differ from guest-worker and colonial programs in two important ways. First, foreign investment is not a program of a representative governing body; private corporations actually do the investment, though, as we have seen, their actions occur within a greater global economic context. Second, foreign investment is not based on the same explicitly racist premises as guest-worker and colonial programs. Private corporations are motivated by profit; they build export-oriented factories in the developing world because it is profitable to do so.

At the same time, private corporations, in assessing potential locations for factories, can be accused of reducing humans to commodities. In chasing the lowest possible wages and the minimum of governmental protections for workers, these multinational corporations are neglecting what John Paul II termed "the priority of labor over capital."[52] While the distances involved

---

49. Heyer, *Kinship across Borders*, 46–47.
50. Heyer, *Kinship across Borders*, 106–7.
51. Ahn, *Religious Ethics and Migration*, 37.
52. John Paul II, *Laborem exercens* (encyclical letter, Castel Gandolfo, Italy, September

and the legacy of exploitation of the developing world have certainly enabled corporations to reduce labor to a commodity like any other, the trend of commodifying labor long preceded the movement of factories to the developing world. Nevertheless, the actions of private corporations do connect US citizens to Mexican migrants. The actions of private corporations themselves do not occur in a historical or political vacuum; they are themselves responses to both the preexisting relationship between the United States and Mexico and the norms of transnational economic structures. This practice of turning to Mexico for cheap labor has a long history in US-Mexico relations. Likewise, the practice of taking advantage of the cheap labor that Mexico offered in the *maquiladora* zone mirrors in some ways the exploitation of Mexico's labor that had roots in Mexican immigration. The narrative of the relationship between Americans and Mexicans must include and acknowledge these uncomfortable histories.

As in the other histories that we have seen, US citizens deny their relationship with Mexican citizens in their immigration policy. In their exhaustive study of the Mexican-US migration system, Massey and colleagues argue that, before 1986, migration between Mexico and the United States was a stable system with a structure that "minimized the negative consequences and maximized the gains for both countries."[53] However, in 1986 the United States began a program of increasingly harsh and restrictive border-control and immigration policies, premised on an account of migration strongly influenced by the neoclassical paradigm: these harsh measures were thought to be needed to prevent a flood of needy strangers. But rather than sealing the borders, these measures simply increased the risks and costs of seasonally returning to Mexico and then reentering the United States. After 1986, undocumented migrants were less likely to return to Mexico and more likely to stay in the United States and find ways to bring their families to them. Ironically, the harsh border-control measures, while intended to keep undocumented migrants out, have instead contributed to the formation of a permanent community of undocumented migrants.[54] Mexico's entry into GATT—and the subsequent growth of export-oriented factories—coincided with this change in border-control policies in the United States. Though these policies were intended to reduce or eliminate undocumented migra-

---

14, 1981), para. 12, http://w2.vatican.va/content/john-paul-ii/en/encyclicals/documents/hf_jp
-ii_enc_14091981_laborem-exercens.html.

    53. Massey et al., *Beyond Smoke and Mirrors*, 71. I do think that Massey et al. are entirely too sanguine about the guest-worker programs.

    54. Massey et al., *Beyond Smoke and Mirrors*, chap. 5.

tion, they actually increased it because they were proposed in isolation from the narrative of a US-Mexico relationship.

Foreign investment in export-oriented manufacturing can initiate a migration system and establish or entrench social positions where one group exploits another. Although foreign investment can be either encouraged or impeded by governments, the actual investing described here is done by private corporations. In this case, citizens of the United States are stuck with the actions not only of their predecessors but of other private citizens. Even in attempting to build literal and metaphorical walls on the southern border, they cannot escape the unintended consequences of these actions.

The US-Mexican migration system is far more complex than this presentation of foreign aid and economic intervention would suggest. Parts of the United States used to be a part of Mexico; Mexican migration to the United States dates back to the nineteenth century. The US version of a guest-worker program, the *bracero* program, predates by decades the first export-oriented factories at the border. Any updated narrative of the relationship between the United States and Mexico must incorporate all of these layered relationships and interventions. One might expect that, unlike many Western European countries, which do not include migration as a part of their foundational narratives, the United States would have an easier time accepting the narrative of its past and present relationships with Mexican migrants. But that is not the case. From the late Samuel Huntington, who argued that the unprecedented waves of Mexican migration threaten American culture and identity, to more recent debates about border security, Mexican migrants are routinely viewed as foreigners who place American security and values in peril.[55] But the long history of relationship between the United States and Mexico suggests that American identity will be forever intertwined with Mexican identity.

Conclusion: Narratives of Future Possibilities

These explorations of relationships past and present represent only a tiny sliver of relationships between citizens and migrants within each of the countries I have discussed here. Narratives that are faithful to reality will require an exploration of the full historical, political, and social context of each re-

---

55. Samuel P. Huntington, *Who Are We? The Challenges to America's National Identity* (New York: Simon and Schuster, 2004).

lationship. Despite the necessary brevity of the narratives recounted here, there are some ethical features of each that are central to a Christian ethics of migration. The first is that false narratives about relationships abound; they are entrenched in the structures of sin and injustice. They condition how we understand the world and can limit what we are able to see, and thus many of these false narratives between citizens and migrants seem obvious to us. It may seem to be conventional wisdom that Islam is incompatible with a Christian nation (as if Muslims have not been living within Western Christian nations for decades or even centuries) or that "Hispanic values" are incompatible with Anglo-American ones.[56] But better narratives can often run counter to conventional wisdom, and resistance to understanding these relationships the way they really are can be powerful.

The second feature of narratives is that the relationships of the past can have an impact on the relationships of the present, circumscribing our choices. The current citizenry may not choose to colonize another country or initiate a government-sponsored foreign recruitment drive. But citizens today are in some sense stuck with the relationships their predecessors had with the colonized. As Zadie Smith says, "They cannot escape their history any more than you can lose your shadow."[57] However, how we respond to those relationships conditions our present and future relationships. Accordingly, the British citizenry could neither escape their past as a former colonial power nor lose the former colonial subjects arriving on their shores. They did, however, have a choice about how to respond, and they chose to evade the consequences of their history. The current relationships between British ethnic minorities and citizens are the result of not only the relationships of the past but the British public's response to it.

Finally, the future possibilities of these relationships form a part of the narrative. That future is yet to be written, but the link between the past and the present can give some direction concerning how we need to think about future possibilities. The future of these relationships depends in part on our own choices and responses to the present and past. Yet, the choices before citizens are not limitless. The proposal of a twentieth-century British politician to "send them back" was never morally or practically viable. Similarly, the communitarian philosophical position of Michael Walzer and others—that political communities have an almost unlimited right to choose their own members—"misses the moral and practical limits of

---

56. Huntington, *Who Are We?*
57. Smith, *White Teeth*, 385.

self-determination," as I have argued elsewhere.[58] Political communities do not have an unlimited choice about their own members; they must respond to the choices that their predecessors have made. Justice toward migrants, then, depends in part on determining the just response to these relationships.

In this chapter I have suggested that, in some sense, the relationships between migrants and citizens condition the possible choices of action of both. Neither migrants nor citizens have the unlimited and unconstrained autonomy to make the ideal choice, whatever that may be. Rather, both migrants and citizens act only in the context of relationships that are not entirely chosen. This examination of the specific context of various migration systems has shown that these relational contexts are often not ethically neutral, but are often marked by broken or damaged relationships.

The examination of the relationships between citizens and migrants leads to a critical insight about the central question of this book. The question of who has responsibility for migrants must take into account the fact that any discussion of responsibility is not starting from an abstract, neutral place free of the ties of history. Rather, the question of responsibility must be addressed from the reality that citizens and migrants have been in relationship with one another—often for a very long time. Though we did not choose these histories, we cannot dispense with them either. The central question facing the citizens of receiving countries is about how to respond rightly to these inherited relationships.

The idea that our unchosen, inherited relationships demand an ethical response appears in Margaret Farley's presentation of the autonomy and relationality of human beings.[59] Farley retrieves the classical definition of justice as giving each person his or her due. In her account of justice, however, she insists that justice requires "[taking] account of the concrete reality of the one to whom it is due, whether what is relevant in this concrete reality is a contract or a basic human need or the history of a shared commitment or all of the above and more."[60] In other words, though meeting basic human needs is certainly a part of justice, as human rights discourse would suggest, so is the complete relational reality of the person. As Farley takes pains to point out, this relational reality is not something that is entirely chosen. It includes networks of historical relationships.

58. Rajendra, "The Rational Agent or the Relational Agent," 365.
59. Farley, "A Feminist Version of Respect for Persons."
60. Farley, "A Feminist Version of Respect for Persons," 184.

This relational reality is often the result of entrenched structures of sin that have brought us into relationship with people all over the world. The structures that have generated migration systems are just one example of these kinds of relationships; and every time we buy clothes or coffee, we participate in these structures.[61] Part of the project of justice, then, is figuring out not what we would owe others in an ideal world, abstracted away from these structured relationships, but figuring out how to justly respond to the relationships in which we find ourselves.

For Further Reading

I can recommend no greater book about the complex interactions between migrants and citizens, past and present, than British novelist Zadie Smith's *White Teeth* (New York: Random House, 2000).

For a history of the German guest-worker program, see Rita Chin's *The Guestworker Question in Postwar Germany* (Cambridge: Cambridge University Press, 2007). Cindy Hahamovitch's account of Jamaican guest workers in the United States, *No Man's Land* (Princeton: Princeton University Press, 2011), and her analysis of "deportable labor," is a breathtaking structural analysis of guest-worker programs.

For an account of migration from Mexico to the United States, see Mark Overmeyer-Velazquez's edited collection *Beyond La Frontera* (Oxford: Oxford University Press, 2011).

For a history of the *bracero* program and its connection to the creation of the *maquiladora* zones in the 1980s and 1990s, see Oscar Martinez's chapter in the Overmeyer-Velazquez collection, entitled "Migration and the Border, 1965–1985."

61. Young, *Responsibility for Justice*, chap. 5.

CHAPTER 4

Theories of Justice in Global Perspective

Contemporary discussions of justice focus on questions of distributive justice, often defined as the normative distribution of benefits and burdens among citizens of a commonwealth. John Rawls, whose book *A Theory of Justice* (1971) reignited contemporary debates about justice, specifically formulated his theory of justice for a "bounded society" that members "enter only by birth and exit only by death."[1] But the bounded society has never existed. Migrants, refugees, and travelers have always crossed borders. In addition, in an increasingly globalized world, in which people not only cross borders but engage with each other across borders, theories of justice must address these relationships. How can we distribute goods justly when the context is not a closed society but the whole world, embedded in webs of complex relationships that began decades or centuries ago? The relationships between migrants and citizens described in the last chapter illustrate some of the complexities that characterize these relationships, but such complex relationships are not limited to migrations.

I have argued that the central question is not who has what rights, but who is responsible for protecting the rights of whom. The philosophical theories of justice that I discuss in this chapter represent the attempts of three schools of thought—*contractarian, deontological,* and *capabilities*—to develop theories of justice that respond to the challenges of transnational justice. In doing so, they all touch on that central question of who bears the responsibility to protect human rights. While only one of them touches directly on the phenomenon of migration, all three theories attempt to hold the universality of human rights in tension with the reality that not every

---

1. John Rawls, *Political Liberalism*, expanded ed., Columbia Classics in Philosophy (New York: Columbia University Press, 2005), 12.

person in the world can bear equal responsibility for protecting the human rights of every other person in the world. In addition, each of these theorists is aware of the dense networks of structural injustice, or sin, that threaten the human rights of the most vulnerable peoples in the world. However, each theory relies on an account of justice as universal moral norms, leaving little room for the particularities and ambiguities of relationships. These theories, I argue, point us toward an account of justice that can integrate the universal moral norms and structural perspectives presented here with an account of justice that can integrate the narratives of particular relationships.

A Contractarian Approach

John Rawls's seminal theory of justice—justice as fairness—specifies principles of justice for a liberal democratic society. A society is defined as a system of cooperation in which members are better off together than they would be alone.[2] Rawls's two principles of justice come from a thought-experiment in which members of these societies imagine themselves behind a "veil of ignorance," which shields them from all knowledge of their particular social locations, talents, or inherited wealth or privilege (Rawls, 17–22, 137). In this "original position," members will come to agree that the following principles of justice should govern society: (1) the equal liberty principle, (2a) the equal opportunity principle, and (2b) the difference principle (Rawls, 60).

These principles stem in part from Rawls's conviction that there will always be a kind of "natural" inequality in every society: people will always be born with different natural talents, to parents of unequal wealth and status in society (Rawls, 102). This unequal distribution of talent and social position is "neither just nor unjust. These are simply natural facts. What is just or unjust is the way that institutions deal with these facts" (102). The principles of justice are meant to constrain these natural inequalities so that they do not result in political or economic injustice. In the original position, no one will know whether he or she will end up on the bottom of the social hierarchy, with few natural talents to help out.

In this thought-experiment, citizens would want access to basic civil and political liberties, no matter where they might find themselves once the veil of ignorance is lifted. No one can trade his or her civil or politi-

2. Rawls, *A Theory of Justice*, 4. Hereafter, page references to this work appear in parentheses within the text.

cal liberties for better economic distribution. Thus, the first principle—the *equal-liberty* principle—is "lexically prior" to the second principle (Rawls, 151–52). The second principle—the *equal-opportunity* principle—states that "offices and positions be open to all." Educational and career opportunities should be open to all regardless of wealth or social position. Finally, the *difference* principle, which manages economic inequality in society, states that inequalities are acceptable as long as they are to the advantage of the least well-off in society.[3] Rather than eliminate economic inequality completely, which would be impossible without violating the first two principles, Rawls says that economic inequality is acceptable as long as the position of the least well-off in society is maximized.

In contrast to classical and medieval definitions of justice as a virtue that belongs to persons, Rawls opens *A Theory of Justice* by saying that "Justice is the first virtue of *social institutions*" (3, emphasis added). These principles of justice as fairness apply not to persons but to the "basic structure" of society, "the way in which the major social institutions distribute the fundamental rights and duties and determine the division of advantages of social cooperation." The institutions that make up the basic structure of society include social, economic, and political institutions like markets, schools, and legal systems (7).[4] In other words, these institutions should be structured according to the two principles of justice so that they both protect the civil and political liberties of citizens and manage natural inequalities.

While many political philosophers have attempted to extend the difference principle to address global inequalities, Rawls is quite clear that the principles of justice as fairness only apply within liberal, democratic societies, not across societies.[5] Within liberal, democratic societies, members share a common understanding of the person as free and equal. Because these societies are in a sense voluntary—members understand that they are better off together than they would be alone—members also share a common understanding of their reciprocal responsibilities to one another. Chief among these responsibilities is the duty to use their talents and resources

3. John Rawls, *Justice as Fairness: A Restatement*, ed. Erin Kelly (Cambridge, MA: Harvard University Press, 2001), 42–43.

4. Iris Marion Young argues that Rawls's account of the basic structure is "vague, ambiguous, and shifting" because Rawls wrongly thinks of structures as a small part of society, rather than a set of social-structural processes that underlie every part of social life (Young, *Responsibility for Justice*, 64–74).

5. See, e.g., Charles R. Beitz, *Political Theory and International Relations* (Princeton: Princeton University Press, 1979).

to benefit the least advantaged in society. This fairly substantial account of responsibilities has no counterpart in Rawls's account of global justice.

The whole world, according to Rawls, simply is not such a voluntary society. Accordingly, the "law of peoples," Rawls's account of global justice, yields substantially weaker responsibilities than justice as fairness. The principles of the law of peoples emerge from the international version of Rawls's thought-experiment, in which representatives of the world's peoples come together in the original position to decide on the principles of global justice. Rather than restating all the principles of the law of peoples here, I will highlight some of the basic ideas that form the backbone of these eight principles.[6] Rawls upholds the traditional ideas of communal self-determination, human rights, just war, and reciprocity. Communal self-determination, which in most formulations derives from the liberal idea of autonomy, is the foundation of principles 1 and 4, which state that the freedom and independence of peoples is to be respected, and that they are protected from unnecessary interference in their internal affairs. Communal self-determination is, however, restricted by the idea of human rights (principle 6), and by the idea of just war, which limits both the cause and the methods of war (principles 5 and 7). In addition, the society of peoples is bound by the idea of reciprocity; peoples must honor treaties and agreements, and can expect other peoples to do the same (principles 2 and 3).

The duty of assistance, the eighth principle of the law of peoples, addresses Rawls's position on the duties of the political community to the world's least-advantaged peoples. While within a society, members have fairly stringent responsibilities to the political community, across borders that separate societies, the duty of assistance represents the highest duty that peoples have towards other peoples. This duty is the responsibility of liberal societies toward "burdened" societies, that is, societies that "lack the political and cultural traditions, the human capital and know-how, and the material and technological resources to be well-ordered."[7] In other words, burdened societies are societies where not all the basic rights of every citizen are respected.[8] The reasons that these societies are not well ordered may vary. Perhaps they lack a tradition of liberalism. Perhaps illiteracy is high, making it more difficult to attain the base-line level of political participation needed to sustain liberal institutions. Perhaps they must cope with frequent

6. For the full eight principles, see Rawls, *Law of Peoples*, 37.

7. Rawls, *Law of Peoples*, 106.

8. See Rawls's definition of the well-ordered society in Rawls, *Justice as Fairness*, 8–9.

natural disasters, making their first priority survival, not the creation of just institutions.

The duty of assistance requires that liberal societies help burdened societies become societies with institutions that are just and respect the basic rights and liberties of their people.[9] Rawls emphasizes that the purpose of this duty of assistance is not to reduce or eliminate inequality, nor even to maintain a minimal standard of living for the people of burdened societies. The duty of assistance requires financial aid only when and only for as long as it will help a burdened society become well ordered. Ideally, all societies should be able to manage their own affairs and in doing so become well-ordered peoples themselves.[10]

This does not mean that Rawls is unconcerned with the material needs of members of burdened societies. Rawls argues that starvation and poverty are inseparable from the political, economic, and social institutions of societies. Once societies have enough support from liberal societies to become well ordered, their institutions will be more just, making chronic poverty unlikely.[11] Rawls's argument for the duty of assistance can be interpreted as an admirable commitment to the principles of nonintervention and self-determination, which are indeed two of the principles of the law of peoples. As long as peoples have the political institutions to be stable, then they should be independent enough not to have to rely on charity of other peoples in perpetuity. They should be able to flourish with the natural and human resources within their territory.

Thus, while members of a society have significant responsibilities to one another, particularly to the least-advantaged in their midst, members of a society do not have these same responsibilities to outsiders. Peoples have responsibilities to other peoples as a whole, but these responsibilities are confined to assisting other peoples to become well ordered so that they can govern themselves without further intervention. Migration—mentioned just once in *The Law of Peoples*—is solely the result of peoples' "failure to regulate their numbers or care for their land."[12] When there are too many people to

---

9. Rawls, *Law of Peoples*, 108–11.

10. Rawls, *Law of Peoples*, 111.

11. In response, Pogge raises the objection that poverty makes countries vulnerable to exploitation from more powerful countries. While Rawls is correct that corruption breeds poverty, poverty also breeds corruption. In any case, the reasons for political corruption are far more complicated than Rawls suggests here. Thomas Pogge, "An Egalitarian Law of Peoples," *Philosophy and Public Affairs* 23, no. 3 (1994): 213.

12. Rawls, *Law of Peoples*, 8.

feed or employ, or when the land is overgrazed and cannot provide enough food for the population, a population must migrate to survive. Immigration, along with poverty, war, and starvation, would disappear in an international society made up of decent and liberal peoples.

As we have seen, Rawls is not alone in presuming that migration is driven by poverty, unemployment, and hunger. However, migration is not the only problem of global justice that is either ignored or misconstrued in the law of peoples. As many have noted, Rawls presumes a world of peoples who have no contact or prior relationship with each other. The global economic system is invisible in the law of peoples. Colonial and quasi-colonial interventions are treated as deviations from the ideal, but ones that do not appear to have any relationship to the present-day global distribution of wealth and power.[13] Rawls's neglect of these challenges to global justice is only possible because of his methodology of ideal theory. Both justice as fairness and the law of peoples use an ahistorical methodology that deliberately sidesteps the complex and messy relationships that individuals and peoples have with one another. For Rawls, in order to envision the ideal, one must abstract from the concrete. However, as I have suggested in chapter 3, if the historical relationships between peoples have some bearing on their responsibilities to each other in the present, then ideal theory obscures rather than illuminates our responsibilities to each other.

Another shortcoming of the law of peoples is that only "peoples" as larger bodies bear responsibilities to other peoples; individuals do not appear to bear these responsibilities. This is perhaps the result of Rawls's reliance on the social contract of a society as a key category for distributing responsibilities. In the absence of a social contract, responsibilities are minimal at best. However, the absence of social contracts does not preclude relationships among peoples, among individuals and peoples, and between individuals. Because these relationships are so often shaped by structural sin, they are often the locus of injustice.

Thus there is no way to apply the law of peoples to an interdependent, globalized world; there is no way to specify what responsibilities individuals have to those who might be members of other peoples; and there is no apparent role for any actors other than peoples and their representative governments. The actors that we have seen in migration-systems theory, specifically multinational corporations and private citizens, seem not to have specific responsibilities to outsiders under the law of peoples. Or if these

13. Rawls, *Law of Peoples*, 53–54.

agents do have responsibilities, they discharge them through their representative governments.

Deontological Ethics

A deontological approach to the problems of global justice is best illustrated by the work of British philosopher Onora O'Neill, who uses the basic framework of the ethics of Immanuel Kant to tackle problems of global justice. I have discussed O'Neill's criticisms of human rights discourse in chapter 1; but O'Neill's work also proposes constructive solutions that fit within her framework of deontological ethics.

Unlike Rawls, who depends on social contracts to differentiate between responsibilities to fellow members and responsibilities to nonmembers, O'Neill fixes the "scope of moral concern" across borders by arguing that moral concern should be extended to everyone with whom an agent is connected.[14] In other words, agents act upon others, either directly or indirectly; such action is only possible because of a connection between two agents. Where such connection exists, there exists also moral obligation. There is no obligation in the absence of connection, nor, O'Neill argues, would there need to be. We cannot be obligated to people who live on a distant island, isolated from us by every personal, social, and institutional form of connection. Without these connections, we would not know whether they needed our help, nor could we give help in the absence of connection. In addition to connection, plurality and finitude also demand our moral attention. Plurality is the idea that others are separate from ourselves, and finitude is the recognition that these others are finite, mortal, vulnerable beings who can suffer injury. When she considers questions of global justice, O'Neill's account of the scope of moral concern enables her to extend moral concern beyond the borders of nation-states—to discrete, finite others who are vulnerable to our actions.

O'Neill's focus not on rights but on moral obligations breaks with many theorists of justice who begin their reflections by discussing the content of human rights. O'Neill does not disagree with the claim that persons have rights; however, she argues that focusing on *rights* rather than their corresponding *obligations* reduces rights to empty rhetoric. "Nothing can be

14. O'Neill, *Towards Justice and Virtue*, chap. 4. Hereafter, page references to this work appear in parentheses within the text.

claimed, waived, or enforced," she says, "if it is indeterminate where the claim should be lodged, for whom it may be waived, or on whom it could be enforced" (129).

A key question is: Who has the responsibility to protect which rights and of whom? This examination of obligations leads O'Neill to argue that not all supposedly universal rights are, in fact, linked to universal obligations. While negative rights (or liberty rights) are indeed linked to universal obligations, positive rights to goods and services are not. For example, the freedom from interference—in one's speech, in one's choice of associates, or in one's religious practice—is linked to the duty of everyone else not to interfere with another person's freedom (130-31). However, positive rights—to food, water, health care, education—cannot be linked to the same universal obligations. Not everyone in the world can be responsible to provide these things to everyone else; we do not have the "access to one another that universal 'positive' intervention would demand" (130). Furthermore, when a person's negative rights are violated, we can trace the violation of those rights to an agent; however, when a person's right to food or shelter has been violated, exactly who can be held accountable is unclear (132). Without accountability for the violations of positive rights, it makes little sense to claim that universal positive rights are tied to universal positive duties.

Instead, positive rights can only be guaranteed by institutions that provide specific rights to specific persons. O'Neill insists that those who advocate for supposedly universal positive rights must instead focus on the need to establish and hold accountable institutions that are intended to protect the rights of specific others (133). "To institutionalize [rights] is not just to secure the 'backing' of the law and the courts, but to define and allocate obligations to contribute and provide the relevant goods and services, and so to fix the very shape of these rights and obligations" (134). In other words, it is only by assigning institutions to protect the rights of individuals that these rights can be concretely realized. By institutions, O'Neill means not only the states and their governments but a wide variety of social, economic, and political institutions. Institutionalization, she writes, "disrupts any simple symmetry of rights and obligations by dispersing obligations, and sometimes rights, across a plurality of agents, officials, and institutions" (135). For example, the right of a person in the United States to health care might be linked to obligations of the states, federal government, insurers, and health-care providers.

As for positive rights, because they cannot be matched by universal obligation, they cannot be universal. They are what O'Neill calls "distributively universal special rights"—universal in that every person should have these rights protected, but special (the opposite of universal) in that they are linked not to universal duties but to the duties of specific actors or institutions (136).

O'Neill's account of justice thus focuses on the principles that should guide and bind institutions. Following Kant, she argues that only those principles that can be universalized should be used to structure institutions, for example, the principle of the rejection of direct and indirect injury. This seemingly thin principle leads to a surprisingly thick account of the role of institutions. The subjects of justice are a plurality of connected, finite, and vulnerable others, "whose social connection and capabilities are formed and fed by the natural and man-made world" (178–80). In other words, the obligation to avoid or reject injury can be connected with a host of positive rights and social conditions that protect the capabilities of embodied and connected vulnerable agents. Though O'Neill never provides a complete list, she intimates that these rights and social conditions include civil and political rights, the avoidance of great disparities of power, and access to positive goods and services.

O'Neill's focus on institutions guides her turn toward the questions of global justice that political philosophers have found so vexing. Because the scope of moral concern crosses borders, so should institutions of all kinds. These transnational institutions must also be structured according to the principles of the avoidance and limitation of injury. Thus, such institutions should avoid—or at least minimize—violence, coercion, and deception.[15] The current state of the world requires just institutions, as well as just transactions, that can limit the vulnerabilities of agents. Global justice, O'Neill argues, thus requires global institutions that span the borders of nation-states. Any institution that can affect others must be bound by the principles of the rejection and limitation of injury of finite and vulnerable others. Existing institutions must be reformed according to these principles.

While O'Neill never addresses the ethics of migration directly, she does write about the role of transnational institutions in constraining states according to these universal principles of obligation. In other words, the foreign and economic policies of states must conform to the principles of the avoidance of injury. Similarly, states must compensate for the avoidable injury that might result from exclusion:

15. O'Neill, *Bounds of Justice*, chap. 7.

If a system of states is to reject avoidable injury it will have to construct institutions which compensate for any systematic or gratuitous injuries created by the exclusion which states practice, and by the varied sorts of dependence they buttress. Where exclusion is a source of avoidable systematic or gratuitous injury, justice will then demand at least that basic human rights and some sorts of economic support be made effective beyond borders, and that asylum and immigration be made available when these fail.[16]

That is to say, O'Neill accepts that the division of the world into sovereign nation-states results in systemic and avoidable injury. Though she does not give examples of what kinds of injury she has in mind, we can speculate that this might include the practices of detention and deportation of migrants that are the inevitable result of a sovereign state's right to choose its own members. Or perhaps she has in mind the very real harms facing would-be economic migrants and political refugees in their own countries.

However morally problematic the existence of borders is, O'Neill pronounces, a world without borders—a world with one state—would risk concentrating too much power in one place.[17] Therefore, borders are necessary; yet they also exclude and injure. Her solution to this quandary is to posit that exclusion itself can be a form of connection to others. But when it is not possible to protect human rights across borders in any other way, immigration and asylum can be a last resort, available when other institutions have failed to prevent injury. This last resort, however, will not necessarily be a rare one, since borders "invariably" exclude, and since this exclusion is often a source of both systemic and gratuitous injury.[18]

O'Neill's reservations about the discourse of human rights and her focus on obligations that can and do cross borders are able to respond to some of the thick, complex relationships described in the preceding chapter. Labor markets, migrant networks, and the policies and institutions of nation-states themselves are all institutions that create connections across borders. In proposing these principles of the avoidance of injury, O'Neill is correctly pointing out that these institutions can be made to more effectively protect the human rights of the people in their scope of moral concern. However,

16. O'Neill, *Towards Justice and Virtue*, 173.
17. O'Neill, *Bounds of Justice*, 200.
18. O'Neill, *Bounds of Justice*, 201.

I find that O'Neill's emphasis on these thin, universalizable principles ultimately falls short.

Obviously, institutions are necessary for the provision of goods that protect positive human rights. In a globalized, interconnected world, states cannot be the only institutions that play a role in protecting the rights of migrants. O'Neill's insistence on the universal principle of the rejection of injury, however, is insufficiently thick to provide actual guidance about who should protect the human rights of migrants. Mario Castro, whose story opens chapter 1, is served by an institution—the shelter at the US-Mexico border run by the Catholic church. But he is left out of the obligations of the governments of the United States and Mexico. Though he is a citizen of Guatemala, his government has no territorial sovereignty in Sonora, Mexico. Perhaps O'Neill would consider this a case where exclusion itself is harming Castro and others like him, and because of this injury, either the United States or Mexico should admit them as full citizens. Or perhaps some other institution, either the Guatemalan state or a transnational nongovernmental organization, should have ensured that Castro never needed to emigrate in the first place in order to survive. But these questions are left open, according to O'Neill's principles. Of all these possible actors, which ones are failing in their responsibility to provide for Castro? To put it another way, O'Neill's insistence on the role of institutions does not help us sort out which institution should be responsible for protecting Castro's rights. The ethical task of allocating these "distributively universal special obligations" remains.

Part of the limitation of O'Neill's approach comes from the limitations of the Kantian deontology that forms her methodological framework. Although O'Neill specifically says that universal principles do not necessarily demand uniform action, with only general universal principles that guide action, it is difficult to see which institutions would bear specific obligations to provide specific goods for specific groups of people.[19] In addition, the spareness of these universal principles leaves no room for responsibilities based on the specific relationships I have described in chapter 3. O'Neill specifically rejects compensatory justice based on past harm:

> To claim special rights we must show a special relationship; but the causal
> links between specific individuals or institutions who injured and were
> injured, or who now injure others and suffer injuries, are too often not

19. O'Neill, *Towards Justice and Virtue*, 136–37.

clear enough to allocate rights of compensation: without allocation, rights are only the rhetoric of manifestos.[20]

O'Neill's claim that the only special relationship that can exist between two parties is a relationship of causal injury is curious, especially given that all kinds of connections across borders lead to expansions in the scope of moral concern. In other words, in expanding the scope of moral concern across borders, O'Neill is specifically arguing that obligations also cross borders. But "connection" is surely not limited to injury, and special relationships are surely not only those that are based on compensation for past harms. The relationships between contemporary citizens and the descendants of guest workers, or between British citizens and the current wave of migrants from South Asia, might not fall into the category of relationships in which one party has harmed another. But that does not mean that there is no other way of understanding the relationship than the responsibilities that emerge from it. While O'Neill's critique of human-rights approaches is helpful, her solution of having institutions structured according to universal principles of the rejection of injury does not solve the problems of how to allocate special obligations to protect special rights in the current global context.

A Capabilities Approach

The third perspective on problems of global justice that I will discuss here is Martha Nussbaum's *capabilities* approach, which Nussbaum presents as a solution to some of the most pressing problems of global justice.[21] Developed as an alternative to measures of aggregate well-being such as per capita GDP, the capabilities approach argues that the central question of justice is: "What is each person [actually] able to do and to be?"[22] The capabilities approach focuses on the dignity and value of each person as an end, while attempting to remain flexible to differences in personal preference and culture. The capabilities are central things that the humans are able to do, should they choose to do them. Each person should be able to develop these capabilities and to have the choice about whether and how to use them. The capabilities

20. O'Neill, *Bounds of Justice*, 132.
21. Nussbaum, *Frontiers of Justice*. Hereafter, page references to this work appear in parentheses within the text.
22. Nussbaum, *Creating Capabilities*, 18.

are irreducible (i.e., they cannot be reduced to one measure) and nontransferable from one person to another.[23]

In response to O'Neill's critique that approaches like Nussbaum's, which assign rights or capabilities to people without specifying who has the responsibility of developing or protecting the capabilities of specific people, Nussbaum argues that duty-based approaches like O'Neill's neither solve the problem of allocation, nor can they provide an account of what people truly need (*Frontiers*, 275–78).[24] Unlike O'Neill, who insists that positive rights can only be tied to special—not universal—duties, Nussbaum argues that because human entitlements are universal, human obligations are as well. "[W]e are all," according to Nussbaum, "under a collective obligation to provide the people of the world with what they need" (280). Focusing on duties rather than rights, Nussbaum argues, is likely to make us "throw up our hands when we reach a problem that looks unwieldy" (281). But starting from entitlements makes the problems of others our own (280).

Nussbaum does not sway from her insistence that the moral duties are ultimately located in individuals. But she does allow that these duties can be derivatively assigned to institutions (307). Because they have organizational and cognitive powers that individuals do not possess, institutions can more effectively address and possibly solve global problems. In addition, since having the freedom to pursue one's own life plays such a central role in the capabilities approach, Nussbaum posits that, only if individuals can discharge their universal obligations through institutions, can they have the freedom and the resources to pursue their own interests (309). Thus, despite Nussbaum's significant theoretical differences with O'Neill, she reaches a similar conclusion in insisting on the importance of institutions in securing global justice.

Like O'Neill, Nussbaum rejects a world state and instead envisions a plurality of institutions—economic institutions, multinational corporations, and NGOs—that can protect capabilities (314–15). Despite her insistence

---

23. Nussbaum, *Creating Capabilities*, 35–36.

24. I am not entirely sure that O'Neill would disagree that some account of human rights and/or capabilities is required for a full account of justice. In fact, she refers to such rights and capabilities herself (O'Neill, *Towards Justice and Virtue*, 170, 173). Elsewhere, she draws on Kant's portrayal of humans as both autonomous and capable of action and "finite and mutually vulnerable, dependent on material resources and not always well disposed to one another" (O'Neill, *Bounds of Justice*, 138). This emphasis on both the agential capacities of the person and the person's embodied and vulnerable nature gives O'Neill an account of obligation that leaves her not too far from Nussbaum.

that global institutions have a role to play, Nussbaum's emphasis remains on the sovereign nation-state as the institution that is primarily responsible for protecting the capabilities of its members. This national sovereignty has "moral importance, as a way people have of asserting their autonomy, their right to give themselves laws of their own making" (314). She emphasizes the moral import of national sovereignty: the nation-state has a primary role in protecting and promoting human capabilities. While rich nation-states, other institutions, and individuals all have duties to aid poorer nation-states, the nation-state and its institutions bear the responsibility not only of protecting the human rights of their members but of deciding what the protection of the central capabilities will look like in a particular context (314). In addition, military force and economic coercion available only to sovereign nation-states serve as last resorts for the most serious and intractable of human rights abuses.[25]

In her writings on global justice, Nussbaum never directly addresses migration. Two of Nussbaum's books on the capabilities approach open with the story of Vasanthi, a Gujarati woman who is able to use many of the capabilities because of the assistance of a nongovernmental institution, which gives her a low-interest loan; the loan in turn helps her secure her economic independence.[26] When Nussbaum discusses poverty in India, it is clear how her account of responsibilities in the capability approach would play out: everyone in the world has a duty to Vasanthi and other women like her, those who live without being able to exercise their minimum of human capabilities.[27] However, these duties could be discharged via institutions: governments—of India, and of Vasanthi's home state of Gujarat—and nongovernmental organizations all have roles to play in protecting her capabilities. Individuals around the world could discharge their responsibilities to her through charitable contributions to the NGO or through the foreign-aid programs of their own governments.

The capabilities approach thus has an elegant solution to some of the problems of global justice. However, when the practical issue at hand is the protection of the rights of migrants, it is not as clear how the capabilities approach would play out. Nussbaum's insistence on both the universality of duties and on the sovereignty of the nation-state creates problems for the rights of migrants. Though Nussbaum does not directly link the right to

---

25. Nussbaum, *Creating Capabilities*, 211.
26. Nussbaum, *Creating Capabilities*, 3.
27. Nussbaum, *Creating Capabilities*, chap. 1.

choose the members of one's own community to the communal right of a nation to self-determination, this direction has been taken by a number of other political philosophers.[28] In other words, national sovereignty is usually taken to include not only the right of a people to choose their own laws but also to choose who their compatriots will be. The right of a nation to set immigration policy also provides an important safeguard against colonization via migration.[29]

On the other hand, the universal duty to ensure the capabilities of everyone in the world suggests that governments have the duty to protect the capabilities of individuals regardless of their citizenship. Indeed, Nussbaum never limits the duties of governments solely to their own citizens; she is careful to say that governments have this duty toward people. In addition, Nussbaum insists that the poor and disadvantaged should occupy a central place in the concerns of the international community, in particular, and "all those who are not themselves unusually burdened" (*Frontiers*, 320). The centrality of the poor and disadvantaged in this global application of the capabilities approach suggests that Nussbaum would probably reject the idea that national sovereignty includes an unrestricted right to choose the members of a political community.

Nussbaum's omission of issues of migration, however, suggests a larger problem with her work: she does not take seriously the inevitability of conflicting obligations, the likelihood that people might not be able to discharge their duties toward all of the poor in the world, and that scarcity imposes compromises in decisions about entitlements. In short, the capabilities approach runs into some of the same problems that Catholic social teaching on migration does.

In addition, while Nussbaum is fully aware that the present distribution of wealth among peoples is in part the result of historical injustice and in part the result of current inequalities in wealth and power in the global economy, these injustices, for Nussbaum, do not give nations or institutions particular responsibilities. Instead, they form another reason to support global redistributive policies through the foreign aid programs of wealthy governments.[30] To put it another way, the particularity of these injustices and the relationships they form do not have much of a role to play in Nussbaum's

---

28. See, e.g., Walzer, *Spheres of Justice*, chap. 2; Rawls, *The Law of Peoples*; David Miller, *National Responsibility and Global Justice* (Oxford: Oxford University Press, 2007), chap. 8.

29. This point comes from a conversation with Daniel Kanstroom.

30. Nussbaum, *Creating Capabilities*, 115–17.

approach. Rather, they are yet another grounding of universal obligations. But we have seen that migration systems are not the evenly distributed results of poverty and unemployment; they are the result of very particular relationships. Exclusionary immigration policies are likewise not the result of a failure of universal obligations, but a failure of particular obligations that result from ignorance of particular histories. The lack of particularity in Nussbaum's approach cannot account for this ignorance, nor the racism and ethnocentrism that often accompany such ignorance.

Conclusion

Despite their methodological differences, the three theories I have examined in this chapter make two important contributions to discussions of justice and human rights. First, all three of the theories of global justice emphasize the importance of universal moral norms—such as human rights and duties. The idea that there is a minimal set of social, material, and political goods that humans require in order to live a dignified life is one that must figure prominently in any account of justice. The second contribution of these theorists is that each attends to the structural dimension of justice. In other words, it is not enough for individuals to treat one another justly; economic, political, and social institutions must be structured in order to provide for and protect individuals' capabilities and rights.

At the same time, all three of these approaches fail to account for the actual historical relationships that have brought migrants and citizens together. None of them is ignorant of these relationships: John Rawls acknowledges the histories of domination of weaker countries by the more powerful; Onora O'Neill argues that the webs of relationships are, in fact, too complicated to be the source of special responsibilities to specific peoples; and Martha Nussbaum uses these kinds of relationships to buttress her calls for foreign aid. But the fact that none of them turns to the specifics of these relationships for an account of responsibilities leads me to believe that it is the very framework of contemporary discussions of justice that makes it difficult to incorporate the narratives of relationships: that is to say, liberal theories of justice have emphasized the universal and uniform nature of these norms; communitarian theories of justice have emphasized that, because moral norms emerge from shared values, they cannot be universal. Most theorists of global justice, including O'Neill and Nussbaum, have rejected communitarianism as too parochial for a globalized world in which we regularly act on and are acted on by people outside our own society.[31] However, in rejecting communitarianism, they have committed themselves to moral principles that must be vague enough to be universal.

The phenomenon of migration that I have described in chapters 2 and 3 suggests that these universal moral norms are not adequately sensitive to the specific narratives of relationships between migrants and citizens. Yet the norms of human rights, capabilities, universal duties, and structural justice should not be easily or lightly discarded either.

So what kind of theory of justice can address the relationships between migrants and citizens? Such a theory of justice must attend to the particularities of historically embedded relationships. It must be attuned not only to the rights of those with no membership in the political community, but to the responsibilities of individuals and institutions to protect human rights. Finally, such a theory of justice must theorize the connection between relationships and responsibilities. In the words of Cristina Traina, the very "fogginess" of these relationships obscures our responsibilities and the just response.[32] Such a theory of justice must take this fogginess as its starting point.

For Further Reading

A quick, thorough, and eminently readable introduction to both philosophical and theological theories of justice is Karen Lebacqz's *Six Theories of Justice* (Minneapolis: Augsburg, 1986).

Thomas Pogge and Darrel Moellendorf's edited collection *Global Justice: Seminal Essays* (St. Paul, MN: Paragon House, 2008) contains essays from many philosophical perspectives.

While this chapter focuses on thinkers who conceptualize justice as universal principles, another strand of thinking on justice insists that justice—indeed all moral norms—is unintelligible apart from the communities in which those norms are developed and practiced. This school of thought, known as communitarianism, is exemplified in Michael Walzer's *Spheres of Justice* (New York: Basic Books, 1983).

---

31. E.g., O'Neill, *Bounds of Justice*, 121.

32. Cristina L. H. Traina, "Facing Forward," in *Distant Markets, Distant Harms: Economic Complicity and Christian Ethics*, ed. Daniel K. Finn (Oxford: Oxford University Press, 2014).

CHAPTER 5

Justice as Fidelity to the Demands of a Relationship

The final two chapters of this book contain my constructive proposal for a theory of justice that responds to the relationships between migrants and citizens. And I begin, as many others before me have, by examining the biblical legal materials about the resident alien that are found in the Hebrew Bible. I argue that these legal materials are not meant to stand alone: they fit into an account of justice that is rooted in the relationship between God and Israel and the complex of historical relationships among God, Israel, and the various strangers in the biblical narratives.

Human rights and just structures are key elements in any ethics of global justice, including an ethics of migration. However, an ethics of migration must be able to respond to the complex and messy relational reality that characterizes migration. In order to respond to the relational reality of migration systems, we need a relational account of justice. The Hebrew Bible defines justice not in terms of abstract norms but in relational categories. While there is no unified and consistent meaning of justice in the Bible, both the Old Testament legal materials and the message of Jesus in the New Testament indicate that justice in these texts is a relational category rather than an objective one.[1] Gerhard von Rad points out that terms like "justice" and "righteousness" in the Hebrew Bible are not about conformity to an abstract ideal but about being true to a specific relationship.[2] Similarly, John Donahue offers a definition of biblical justice as "fidelity to the demands of a

---

1. For a useful survey of the variations of the meaning of justice throughout the Hebrew Bible and New Testament, see John R. Donahue, "The Bible and Catholic Social Teaching," in Himes et al., *Modern Catholic Social Teaching*.

2. Gerhard von Rad, *Old Testament Theology*, trans. D. M. G. Stalker, vol. 1 (New York: Harper, 1962), 371.

relationship."[3] Both von Rad and Donahue see this idea of justice as coming out of a relational anthropology in which people are "constantly moving in and out of relationships."[4] In the Hebrew Bible the concrete demands of relationships are detailed in the laws of the covenant, which are rooted in Israel's relationship with God.

I will examine a specific set of Hebrew Bible texts to discover how the biblical definition of justice plays out in particular relationships: the legal materials in the Pentateuch on the *gēr*, or resident alien. While there are certain parallels between the social location of the *gērim* in ancient Israel and that of immigrants in Western society today, I am less interested in applying the specifics laws to contemporary secular contexts than in examining how this relational account of justice manifests itself in these laws. The norms governing the relationships between the Israelites and the *gērim* directly reflect the entire relational context of the covenant, in which the history of God's relationship with Israel shapes every other relationship. While these norms do include the central justice concern of contemporary theorists—the just distribution of benefits and burdens in ancient Israel—norms of distribution depend on an accurate appraisal of both the relationship between God and Israel and the relationships among the Israelites and the *gērim* in their midst. Near the end of this chapter I explore how the Hebrew Bible's relational perspective on justice is also reflected in the new covenant of Jesus Christ, which changes relationships between members of the community and strangers. This way of looking at justice offers a model for contemporary discussions of justice that can better respond to the complex relationships that drive migration.

Reading the Bible as a Source for Justice

Before we delve into the biblical texts, a word about my methodology in this chapter is in order. The difficulties inherent in using the Bible as a source for Christian ethics are well documented.[5] The Bible is not a detailed, uniform handbook to the moral life; rather, it is a diverse collection of texts

---

3. John R. Donahue, "Biblical Perspectives on Justice," in *The Faith That Does Justice*, ed. John Haughey (New York: Paulist Press, 1977), 69.

4. Von Rad, *Old Testament Theology*, 371.

5. Bruce C. Birch, *Let Justice Roll Down: The Old Testament, Ethics, and Christian Life* (Louisville: Westminster John Knox, 1991), 41–42. Hereafter, page references to this work appear in parentheses within the text.

that record the experience of different peoples with God. As such, the Bible does not directly address many ethical issues that confront Christians today, including who has responsibility for the human rights of noncitizens. In fact, the Bible does not speak with a unified voice at all; its many texts have their own authors, audiences, and agendas. There is no single "biblical" approach to any theological or ethical issue in the Bible. Even without such varying perspectives and contradictions, it is difficult to bridge the differences in historical, religious, social, and political contexts that separate the biblical contexts, not only from each other, but from our context today. For example, ancient Israel as represented in the Hebrew Bible was intended to be a theocracy that had a God-given covenant as its constitution. Many of the early Christian communities of the New Testament believed that the Second Coming was imminent, obviating the need to reform the social institutions of their day. Both situations are far from the context of the modern liberal democracy, where Christian citizens participate in shaping the laws and policies of secular governments. In addition, many texts of the Bible seem to accept social and political arrangements that many today would find problematic—in some cases even repellent (42–43).

Despite these difficulties, I read the Bible as a unified source with a single perspective on justice that is manifested in the legal materials on the entity of the *gēr*. I do so because, despite the diversity of the texts, Christians believe that the Bible, as a whole, is the word of God. In other words, the Bible can be read as a unified text because the Bible is taken to be a unified source in Christian theology. In the words of Bruce Birch, "in the Bible's drama, its character, its themes, its struggles, its beauty and its complexity we are supplied with much of our vision of life in the world lived in relationship to God" (33). That is, the whole Bible, rather than just a handful of texts, supplies a moral vision for the Christian life. The early church rejected the idea that only parts of the Bible reveal God, instead affirming that both the Hebrew Bible and the New Testament in their entirety reveal God. This method of reading the Bible, grounded in theological claims, is only available to Christians. However, in providing an alternative to contemporary accounts of justice as universal norms, *justice as fidelity to the demands of a relationship* forms the backbone of the account of justice that I develop in the next chapter: justice as responsibility to relationships. This account of justice can inform discussions of migration in a multireligious society.

Reading the Bible as a unified text means that we can read the texts of the Hebrew Bible and the New Testament with an eye to how these texts consider the social category of "resident alien," or "stranger." Many of the various texts in the Hebrew Bible refer to one another. The root verbal form of the noun *gēr* is "to sojourn," a verb used to describe the activities of many of the Israelite forefathers and -mothers. Abraham's slave Hagar is a foreigner in these texts, and her name is also etymologically connected to the word *gēr*. The legal materials directly refer to the Israelites' captivity in Egypt: the word *gērim* is used to describe both the Israelite slaves in Egypt and resident aliens in ancient Israel. The Israelites' liberation from Egypt, of course, is the foundational narrative of the Hebrew Bible. When we read the Hebrew Bible as a unified text, the concept of foreignness or otherness emerges, not as an ancillary concept but one that is central to the Hebrew Bible as a whole.

Although most Christians understand themselves to be released from the Sinai covenant, I argue that these legal materials of the Pentateuch are still central to the Christian story because they are central to the Bible itself. The event of the Exodus, so central to the self-understanding of the people of Israel, is unintelligible without the legal materials, in which God establishes his identity as the anti-pharaoh, in whose land no one will be exploited as the Hebrew slaves were in Egypt. The prophets are constantly calling their people back to the covenant. Therefore, while at first glance the legal materials of the Pentateuch are ancillary to the Christian story, on reflection they are important to Christians because of their importance to the Bible as a whole.

Another methodological choice I consider central to this chapter is to read the New Testament in continuity with the Hebrew Bible. Just as I read the Hebrew Bible as a unified text and look for continuity among the different texts that concern the *gēr*, I see the New Testament as a text that picks up some of the major ethical trajectories of the Hebrew Bible. Even though it reflects the theological, ethical, pastoral, and practical concerns of the earliest Christian communities rather than those of the ancient Israelites, the New Testament maintains the Hebrew Bible's concern for the protection of the stranger.

Of course, in reading the Bible as a unified document, we must still honor the integrity and diversity of the texts themselves. Bruce Birch argues that it is important to find a hermeneutical halfway point between rejecting any attempt to read the Bible as a whole and imposing an artificial unity on the Bible that neglects the diversity of voices (42). In order to find this halfway point, I use the work of historical-critical and social-scientific biblical scholars in order to read the texts in their own context and preserve the diversity of these texts. Thus, my examination of the legal codes acknowledges that the different collections of law have different prescriptions. But I also address the question of what might be common to these different norms regarding the *gēr*.

In drawing on historical-critical scholarship of the Bible, we must also acknowledge that many Bible scholars who use the historical-critical method are quick to point out that these texts concerning the *gēr* may have little or no basis in history. The Exodus event might not have happened at all; there is no archaeological evidence of the Israelites' slavery in Egypt. Likewise, the laws of the Hebrew Bible may never have been practiced as written—or perhaps at all. I am here following Bruce Birch in presuming that, whether or not the events described in the Exodus actually happened, and whether or not the legal codes were actually practiced, these texts still reveal a vision of justice and a blueprint for how the norms of justice might extend to the nonmembers of a society (40–41). In other words, whether or not the texts describe actual events and practices is irrelevant to the account of justice that emerges from them.

The last methodological point involves my decision to focus on the legal materials of the Hebrew Bible rather than on any particular text of the New Testament. I have chosen to do this for three reasons. First, the political circumstances of ancient Israel are more similar to those of democracies today than to those of the New Testament communities. The pre-exilic ancient Israelites had a government of their own that had to determine the ethical import of membership. Their social location was one of relative power. In contrast, the early Christian communities of the New Testament did not have a government of their own. Their own social location was one of dispossession and marginalization; in some cases, they were even persecuted by the imperial power. Being a citizen granted a person privileges in the first-century Roman Empire; however, since Christians themselves were marginalized, even Christians who had citizenship were not in positions of political power.

The second reason I have chosen to focus on the Hebrew Bible texts is that the early Christian communities were not as interested in structurally reforming the social and political institutions of their day. New Testament scholars have speculated that this was because these apocalyptic communities assumed that the institutions of their time were going to pass away. That apocalypticism is reflected in the New Testament authors' reluctance to criticize the Roman Empire; for their communities, institutions such as political membership were irrelevant in a way that they were not for the ancient Israelites.

The third reason for my Hebrew Bible focus is that the New Testament texts are characterized by a certain cosmopolitanism that, while a helpful rejoinder to racism and ethnocentrism, is limited in its ability to answer the central question that emerged from chapters 2 and 3: What is the most appropriate response to the relationships that characterize migration systems? Paul's proclamation that in Christ "there is no longer Greek nor Jew" does challenge ideologies of racial and ethnic superiority that are sometimes used to justify draconian immigration policies.[6] But this cosmopolitanism also makes all *strangers* virtually equivalent in their very lack of relationship to *members*.

Similarly, many who draw on New Testament cosmopolitanism seek to completely attenuate the ethical import of citizenship in a particular nation-state. This approach certainly challenges any view that asserts that immigrants should be cut off from the distribution of social benefits due to their lack of citizenship in a society. However, the narratives of relationships that I presented in chapter 3 suggest that our unchosen national identities may give us inherited responsibilities. Hence, the New Testament cosmopolitanism glosses over the ethical implications of our unchosen participation in specific narratives.

In contrast to the New Testament texts, the legal materials of the Pentateuch are a far more "fitting" source for the ethics of migration than are the New Testament texts. The texts of the Sinai covenant are addressed to a people endowed with membership and a claim to the land they inhabit; yet these texts concern those with no claim to the land. As such, there are striking parallels between the situation of the *gēr* in ancient Israel and the migrant today. While I do not wish to update the ancient legal materials for a contemporary context, examining the parallels between the two groups may help us imagine what "justice as fidelity to the demands of a relationship" might look like today.

The key to this examination is biblical social-scientific scholarship on the *gēr* (plural: *gērim*) in ancient Israel, people who lived under political, economic, and social institutions not their own. Because citizens in liberal democracies shape their political and economic institutions through participation in the democratic process, those who cannot participate — noncitizens — are like the *gērim* of ancient Israel: they cannot participate in the democratic processes that impact them and that would enable them to claim membership in these institutions. Legal migrants, by virtue of having no claim on citizenship in the nation-state, are vulnerable; undocumented

6. See, e.g., Donald Senior, "'Beloved Aliens and Exiles': New Testament Perspectives on Migration," in Groody and Campese, *A Promised Land, a Perilous Journey*, 20–34.

migrants are even more so. Undocumented migrants are vulnerable to precisely the kinds of exploitation that the Israelites suffered in Egypt. Like the Israelites, who sat by the fleshpots of the Egyptian masters, undocumented migrants often live in poverty in lands of plenty. In both cases, the labor of the stranger is unending, dangerous, and without reward. This labor sets them apart from those with full membership.

These similarities between the situation of the *gērim* in the Pentateuch and migrants in contemporary liberal democracies make the legal materials of the Pentateuch an obvious resource for a Christian ethics of migration.[7] These laws are directed toward the members as a warning to avoid the temptation to exploit nonmembers; they are founded on a concept of justice based on obligations in particular relationships. Although the social, political, and religious context of the New Testament is quite different from the Pentateuch, a similar understanding of justice is found in the New Testament as well.

The Hebrew Bible: The *gēr* in the Legal Materials

In the legal materials of the Pentateuch, the noun *gēr* denotes the specific category of a person with special rights and protections in Israel. The legal materials on the *gēr* can be grouped into three categories: (1) commandments that group the *gēr* with other vulnerable groups in ancient Israel, such as the poor, the widow, and the orphan, and ensure economic protection for these very vulnerable groups; (2) commandments that include the *gērim* with the Israelites in purity codes; and (3) general exhortations to treat the *gēr* with love and justice.

The noun *gēr* comes from the Hebrew root verb *gwr*, which means "to sojourn," or "to reside as an alien."[8] Thus the word *gēr* is usually thought to mean someone who is sojourning in another land. In many narrative texts of the Hebrew Bible, the verb *gwr* is used to refer to Israelites fleeing to other

---

7. While there are other texts in the Bible that refer to the status of nonmembers, such as the postexilic texts of Ezra and Nehemiah that command the Israelites to expel their foreign wives, these texts are set in the context of a postexilic community that was trying desperately to maintain/recover its identity after the exile. Given the insights of migration-systems theory, in which large-scale migrations are often the result of actions of the host country, perceiving contemporary migration as a threat to the identity of the nation-state is a misapprehension of contemporary migration. Thus Ezra-Nehemiah is not a context at all analogous to our own.

8. The English New Revised Standard Version translates *gwr* in this way.

lands, to Abraham during his sojourn in Egypt after fleeing famine in Canaan (Gen. 12:10), and to Lot during his flight from the destruction of Sodom and Gomorrah (Gen. 19). The verb is also used when Isaac and Joseph sojourn in Gerar and Egypt due to famine. While the verb *gwr* is generally translated "to sojourn," it usually does not refer to nomads, for whom sojourning is a way of life. Its derivative, the noun *gēr*, is also distinct from the noun *nokri* (often translated "foreigner"), which is used to denote a foreign traveler or someone residing in Israel for a shorter time. This distinction is important because, in the legal materials, the *nokri* does not have the same rights as the *gēr*.[9] Thus, the verb *gwr* connotes an extended residence in a foreign land by someone who has fled his home.[10]

The theories as to the exact identity of the *gēr* are many and varied. Some biblical scholars argue that, far from being a general category of immigrant or refugee, this term was reserved for Israelite refugees from the Northern Kingdom who fled after the downfall of Samaria.[11] Others argue that the term refers to Canaanites who lost their land and property when the Israelites appropriated it, but were allowed to remain as laborers.[12] A third theory proposes that the *gēr* were neither refugees nor immigrants who came to Israel seeking refuge, but non-Israelite proselytes who had attached themselves to Israel for religious reasons.[13] Still others argue that the meaning of the term *gēr* shifts between the narrative texts of the Pentateuch and the Holiness Code, the Covenant Code, and the Deuteronomic Code: thus *gēr* may mean immigrant, resident alien,

9. Ludwig Köhler et al., *The Hebrew and Aramaic Lexicon of the Old Testament* (Boston: Brill, 2001), 700. For examples of laws concerning the *nokri*, see Deut. 14:21; 15:3; 23:20; 29:21.

10. Though the noun *gēr* derives from its verb form, the two are not necessarily equivalent. It has been argued that while the verb form in the narrative texts denotes any sojourner, the noun form in the legal texts is a specific legal category. José E. Ramírez Kidd, *Alterity and Identity in Israel: The [Gēr] in the Old Testament* (New York: Walter de Gruyter, 1999).

11. See Matty Cohen, "Le 'ger' biblique et son statut socio-religieux," *Revue de l'histoire des religions* 207 (1990): 131–38.

12. Johannes Pedersen and Fru Aslaug (Mikkelsen) Møller, *Israel, Its Life and Culture*, vol. 1 (London: Oxford University Press, 1926), 40–41.

13. D. Kellerman, "Gēr, Gur," in *Theological Dictionary of the Old Testament*, vol. 2, ed. G. Johannes Botterweck and Helmer Ringgren (Grand Rapids: Eerdmans, 1974). This argument is based on the inclusion of the *gerim* in the religious festivals and purity regulations of ancient Israel in the Holiness Code. Others refute this argument, countering that the inclusion of the *gērim* in the purity regulations of the Holiness Code stems from a concern with the sanctity of the land that depends on the observance of all its inhabitants. Moshe Weinfeld, *Deuteronomy and the Deuteronomic School* (Winona Lake, IN: Eisenbrauns, 1992), 232.

or proselyte, depending on where the term is found in the Pentateuch.[14] Finally, Roland De Vaux proposes that the population of *gērim* in ancient Israel was probably a mix of Northern Kingdom refugees, non-Israelite immigrants, and Canaanites.[15]

Regardless of the exact composition of the *gērim* population of ancient Israel, these people, whether refugee, Canaanite, or Israelite, were vulnerable because they were living under political, social, and economic institutions not of their own choosing. For non-Israelite *gērim*, this is obvious. The laws of ancient Israel stem from an alien religion, yet these laws would regulate the life of a non-Israelite *gēr*.[16] The non-Israelite would not necessarily have been included in the religious observances and festivals that shaped life in ancient Israel. But even if we posit that the *gērim* were Israelite refugees from the Northern Kingdom who worshiped the same deity who was worshiped in Judah, these refugees would have had to live under different political, social, and economic institutions than the ones they had known in the Northern Kingdom (De Vaux, 97).[17]

Most significantly, Israelite refugee *gērim*, like their non-Israelite counterparts, could not own the land that was so important in agricultural societies. Because the land was given to the Israelites by God, the Israelites could not permanently sell their land (Lev. 25:25). Rather, if an Israelite fell into debt or was no longer able to maintain his land, he was allowed to sell it to his nearest relative in order to keep the land in the family (166–67). Even this sale of the land within family was not permanent, since all land was to be returned to the hands of its original owner during the Year of Jubilee (175).[18] In any case, whether a Canaanite, a non-Israelite alien, or a refugee from the

14. See Theophile James Meek, "The Translation of Ger in the Hexateuch and Its Bearing on the Documentary Hypothesis," *Journal of Biblical Literature* 49 (1930): 172–80.

15. Roland De Vaux, *Ancient Israel: Its Life and Institutions*, trans. John McHugh (Grand Rapids: Eerdmans, 1997). Hereafter, page references to this work appear in parentheses within the text.

16. This is particularly true in the Holiness Code, where the *gērim* are bound by the same purity regulations that bind the Israelites.

17. Although the evidence regarding the institutional practices of the Northern Kingdom is scant, De Vaux makes it clear that Israel and Judah were independent political entities with separate institutional practices (97).

18. De Vaux, *Ancient Israel*, 175. Although there is much debate about whether the Jubilee Year was actually practiced, I argue that the position of the *gēr* would have been vulnerable even if the Jubilee Year was never instituted because, if a *gēr* managed to secure ownership of land, his ownership would have been insecure because it went against the written law of ancient Israel.

Northern Kingdom, the *gēr* would generally not have been able to own land because land was usually sold to the nearest relative.

Because the *gērim* could not own land, they were particularly vulnerable to poverty. Rather than living off their land, they were dependent on wages from employment. The *gērim* and other landless people probably worked as shepherds or agricultural laborers, hired by the day (Lev. 19:13; Deut. 24:15) or by the year (Lev. 25:50) (De Vaux, 76). The irregular nature of their employment and their vulnerability to "unjust masters" accounts for their economic vulnerability. Accordingly, Deuteronomy requires that these laborers be paid daily "because they are poor and their livelihood depends on [their wages]" (Deut. 24:15).

Another indication of the *gērim*'s economic vulnerability is that they were included with the other vulnerable groups that were to be the beneficiaries of agricultural and tithing practices that gave the remains of the harvest to the hungry (Lev. 19:10; 23:22; Deut. 14:28–29; 24:19; 26:12–13). Thus, like the poor, the widows, the orphans, and the Levites, the *gērim*— perhaps due to the seasonal and irregular nature of their employment—were likely to go hungry.

The inclusion of the *gēr* with the widow and orphan in the Deuteronomic triad suggests that, in addition to being economically vulnerable like the widows and orphans, the *gērim* were socially vulnerable as well. *Widows*, having lost their connection to a landed male, were dependent on the charity of relatives. *Orphans* most likely referred to the children of women whose husbands were unknown, poor, or deceased. Like widows, they would not have had ties to a landed man (a father).[19] The inclusion of the *gērim* in the triad may indicate that, like the widow and the orphan, the *gēr* lacked ties not only to land but to kin. If many of the *gērim* were newly arrived refugees from the social, political, and environmental upheavals that broke families apart, they, like widows and orphans, lacked the social protections that a landed family would provide.

As strangers in a strange land, the *gērim* were particularly vulnerable to poverty, hunger, and exploitation. Living under foreign laws and institutions, lacking ties to land and family, the *gērim* experienced some of the same vulnerabilities that strangers experience today. Therefore, the

19. Ramírez Kidd suggests that the Deuteronomic emphasis on the protection of widows and orphans results from the process of urbanization which eroded family ties and left widows and orphans unable to depend on the extended relatives for protection (Ramírez Kidd, *Alterity and Identity in Israel*, 43–45).

laws for the protection of the *gērim* were critical to their survival in a strange land.

Israelites *as* gērim *in the Land of Egypt*

In his exhaustive study of the *gēr* in the Hebrew Bible, José Ramírez Kidd notes that the Pentateuch is unique among the texts of the ancient Near East in its inclusion of the subject of the stranger in its legal texts. While the literatures of Egypt, Mesopotamia, and Ugarit place the poor, widows, and orphans in some combination under the protection of the gods, only the legal codes of Israel extend this same protection to the stranger.[20] In neighboring lands, the exclusion of the stranger from the protection of the gods left that stranger without any rights at all.[21] In contrast, all three collections of law in the Hebrew Bible resound with the command to treat the *gēr* with justice, to love the *gēr*, and to treat the alien as a fellow citizen (Exod. 22:21; 23:9; Lev. 19:33-34; Deut. 10:17-19).

Perhaps these laws are unique to Israel because only Israel had a narrative of its origins as a people living the experience of being *gērim* themselves.[22] The exhortations in the legal materials to treat the *gērim* with justice—and even love the *gērim*—are always followed by the reminder that the Israelites were once strangers themselves in the land of Egypt (Exod. 23:9; Lev. 19:33-34; Deut. 10:19). The very content of the laws protect and include the *gērim* in such a way as to prevent the exploitation that the Israelites suffered in Egypt. The constant evocation of Israel's oppression as *gērim* in the land of Egypt leads Israelites to identify with the *gērim* in their own land. The norms of justice for the *gērim* are thus inseparable from Israel's experience in Egypt and their entire relationship with God.

---

20. Ramírez Kidd, *Alterity and Identity in Israel*, 110-16.

21. Bertholet, quoted in De Vaux, *Ancient Israel*, 113.

22. Kidd argues that the concern for the *gēr* reflects the fact that these texts were either written or edited in exilic or postexilic times. He rejects the argument that these laws stem from Israel's experience in Egypt, arguing that the reminder of *gēr*-hood in Egypt (as opposed to slavery in Egypt) most likely refers to Joseph's sojourn in Egypt, during which he was treated well (Ramírez Kidd, *Alterity and Identity in Israel*, 110-16). I think it unlikely that the evocation to remember *gēr*-hood in Egypt refers to the Egyptians' hospitality, as invocations to remember Egypt are liturgically tied to the Israelites' oppression there and God's liberation. This is not to suggest that the material on the *gēr* is unrelated to the Israelites' experiences of exile later in its history.

The story of Israel in Egypt begins when Joseph was sold into slavery in Egypt by his brothers. By serving as advisor to the pharaoh, Joseph rose to power as governor in Egypt and was afterwards joined by his father's family. During Joseph's lifetime, relations between the Israelites and the pharaoh were good, since Joseph had twice saved Egypt during times of famine. After the death of Joseph, however, a new pharaoh came to power who feared the growing population of Israelites:

> Look, the Israelite people are more numerous and more powerful than we. Come, let us deal shrewdly with them, or they will increase and, in the event of war, join our enemies and fight against us and escape from the land. (Exod. 1:9–10)

Contemporary commentary on the Exodus narrative notes that the pharaoh's reasoning is hardly unique in human history; once we define the "other" as essentially unlike us, and thus a threat to "our" way of life, oppression in the name of self-defense seems necessary and justified.[23]

In order to check the growing Hebrew population, the pharaoh ordered their male infants to be thrown into the Nile; and he put the adults to work as slaves. Michael Walzer points out that, even though contemporary readers are most shocked by the practice of infanticide (indeed, genocide), it is the unending and exhausting labor itself that makes slave life "bitter with hard service" (Exod. 1:13).[24] The pharaoh used labor to punish and humiliate the Israelites; he met any complaint or challenge to his authority with an increase in the difficulty and scope of the work, as when Moses challenged him (Exod. 5:5–14).

Slavery in Egypt was characterized not only by brutal and unending work, but by exclusion from the common wealth that the labor of the slaves had helped to build. Although the Israelites had built supply cities for the pharaoh for emergency grain in times of famine, they themselves went without. As Walzer observes, they lived in close proximity to lives of leisure and luxury without being able to participate.

> The Israelites in Egypt were attracted by Egyptian life and by Egyptian worship, but in neither of these could they fully or freely share. We might

---

23. Michael Goldberg, *Jews and Christians, Getting Our Stories Straight: The Exodus and the Passion-Resurrection* (Philadelphia: Trinity Press International, 1991), 28.

24. Michael Walzer, *Exodus and Revolution* (New York: Basic Books, 1985).

think again about Exodus 16: It does not say, as the Midrash reports, "when we did eat from the flesh pots," but "when we sat by the flesh pots." They had to eat their bread without meat. They smelled the meat, but didn't taste it.[25]

By virtue of their identity as *gērim*, the Israelites were excluded from the benefits and privileges of being Egyptian.

As we know, the story of the Exodus ends not with the triumph of the pharaoh over the Israelites, but with the triumph of God over the pharaoh. In keeping with the Abrahamic covenant, God delivered the Israelites from Egypt and led them through the desert into the Promised Land. The land was not a gift given to the Israelites by God unconditionally; rather, it was entrusted to the Israelites on the condition that they keep the covenant. Laws for the covenant that protected the vulnerable, the widows, orphans, poor, Levites, and the stranger were based on the reminder that God delivered the Israelites from the land of Egypt. In other words, Israel is to be the anti-Egypt, because God is the anti-pharaoh.

The legal materials of the Hebrew Bible thus resound with the statement that Israel is not to behave as Egypt did toward strangers—"for you were once strangers in the land of Egypt" (Lev. 19:34; Exod. 22:20; 23:9; Deut. 10:19). Agricultural laws, for example, protected the *gērim*, along with other vulnerable groups, from hunger (Lev. 19:9–10; 23:22; Deut. 14:28–29; 24:19; 26:12–13). Laws setting limits on work guaranteed that all would have a day of rest.[26] While life in the house of bondage involved unending, exhausting, degrading labor, the *gēr* in Israel, along with all citizens of Israel, was forbidden from doing any work on the Sabbath, giving everyone a rest from the backbreaking labor that characterized agricultural life (Deut. 5:12–14). Similarly, the whole community of Israel—including the *gērim*, the slaves, the poor, widows, and orphans—is commanded to "rejoice before the Lord" during the harvest festivals (Deut. 16:11, 14; Exod. 34:22; Lev. 23:34). Like extending the Sabbath to the *gērim*, including the *gērim* in the harvest festivals gave them not only an opportunity to rest and feast but to participate

---

25. Walzer, *Exodus and Revolution*, 34.

26. Although the Holiness Code includes the *gēr* in the purity regulations of habit and diet that are required to maintain the holiness of the land, the Deuteronomist specifically excludes the *gēr* from certain dietary restrictions of the Israelites (Deut. 14:21). Since this restriction from work on the Sabbath is found in Deuteronomy and not in the Holiness Code, I interpret it as rooted in humanitarian concern for the *gēr* and not a measure to protect the holiness of the land.

in communal celebrations. Neither the *gēr* nor the poor were excluded from these festivities.

Finally, and most strikingly, the Pentateuch gives the *gēr* legal rights in the justice system. Unlike the surrounding cultures, where the *gēr* was without legal rights, the *gēr* in Israel had no disadvantage in disputes with Israelites (Deut. 1:16).[27] The Holiness Code emphasizes that the alien and citizen live under the same law and are judged by the same law for infractions (Lev. 24:22; Num. 15:14).

In its historical context, the concern for the *gēr* in the legal materials of the Pentateuch is striking. Not only are the *gērim* specifically included with the other vulnerable groups as under God's protection, they are protected with specific laws that recognize their specific vulnerability. The *gērim* even have a measure of equality with the Israelite: the *gēr* "shall be to you as the citizen among you" (Lev. 19:34). Although claiming that the *gēr* was the equal of the Israelite would be an overstatement, these laws represent a significant shift from the "clan ethos" that characterized most of the surrounding societies of the time. In ancient Israel, membership was no longer "the ground for just treatment."[28]

The legal materials establish the crucial difference between God and the pharaoh. Had the covenant not included these laws for the protection and inclusion of the *gēr*, God would be just another pharaoh, providing for and protecting his own people, while condemning strangers to lives of misery.[29] But God's election of Israel as the chosen people does not exclude outsiders from God's love; rather, God is said to love the *gēr* (Deut. 10:18). Ultimately, these laws for the *gēr* are rooted in the character of this God who, unlike human rulers, does not seem to love even his chosen people more than outsiders.

27. Ramírez Kidd, *Alterity and Identity*, 55.

28. This phrase comes from Christopher Frey, who argues that ancient Israel was indeed characterized by a clan ethos, in which "membership [was] the ground of the claim for just treatment, and in which the stranger presented an extraordinary problem." Christopher Frey, "The Impact of the Biblical Idea of Justice on Present Discussions of Social Justice," in *Justice and Righteousness: Biblical Themes and Their Influence*, ed. Henning Graf Reventlow and Yair Hoffman, Journal for the Study of the Old Testament Supplement Series 137 (Sheffield, UK: Sheffield Academic Press, 1992), 98. Social-scientific biblical scholarship has also pointed to the ways that social standing in ancient Israel was derived from the standing of one's family and tribe. See Ronald Hendel, *Remembering Abraham: Culture, Memory, and History in the Hebrew Bible* (New York: Oxford University Press, 2005), 34. This argument is problematic when read in the context of the striking protections for the *gēr* in ancient Israel.

29. This point comes from a conversation with Nick Austin, SJ.

Justice, Narratives, and the gērim

God's proclivity to love the outsider is revealed in the Exodus event, in what has been said to be "the first time in human history in which the divine world was seen to side with outlaws, fugitives, and immigrants rather than political structures whose policies and use of power made such social types inevitable."[30] Thus, once God gives the land to the Israelites, it seems inevitable that there will be outsiders: after all, not everyone can be an Israelite. However, God's history of relationship with Israel puts Israel's relationship with the *gērim* residing in Israel into a complicated web. Israel is indeed God's chosen people, and the land is God's gift to Israel. But Israel's history with God is formed by the central events of Exodus, in which the Israelites themselves are *gērim*. Although one would think that, since the *gērim* are foreign, the Israelites and the *gērim* would have no relationship, the biblical texts themselves reject this interpretation: the Israelites have a relationship with the *gērim* because they were once *gērim* themselves. This particular history with God places a relational claim on the Israelites: the claim affects not only the Israelites' relationship with God but the Israelites' relationship with the *gērim* in their own land, and these relationships lead to the responsibilities that the Israelites have toward the *gērim*.

The relationship among God's election of Israel, Israel's identity as *gērim*, and the commandment to love the *gēr* in ancient Israel points to a central irony about the gift of the land to Israel. While God gives the land to the Israelites as his chosen people, living as God's chosen people requires what could be called a preferential option for the non-Israelite. Walter Brueggemann addresses this irony in his exploration of land as both gift and temptation in the Hebrew Bible.[31] As Israel goes from being a wandering band of former slaves in the wilderness to a settled nation with a land of their own, they face the temptation to forget the covenant. Having land represents satiety, comfort, and power, and the satiated, comfortable, and powerful are prey to "the seduction of imagining it was always so, and that Israel made it so."[32] To put it another way, the land, while a gift from God, is also a temptation to forget their relationship with God and the demands that this relationship

30. Frank Spina, "Israelites as *Gerim*," in *The Word Shall Go Forth: Essays in Honor of David Noel Freedman*, ed. Carol L. Meyers and M. O'Connor (Winona Lake, IN: Eisenbrauns, 1992), 332.

31. Walter Brueggemann, *The Land: Place as Gift, Promise, and Challenge in Biblical Faith*, 2nd ed. (Minneapolis: Fortress, 2002).

32. Brueggemann, *The Land*, 52.

places on them. The power that comes with land tempts Israel to forget that they were once powerless strangers in need of God's protection. Forgetting this episode in Israel's historical memory tempts Israel to become another Egypt by using the power of land to increase the wealth of the Israelites at the expense of the strangers.

Brueggemann writes that memory in the form of Torah is a weapon against the temptation of the landed to forget.[33] Accordingly, the Pentateuch is laced with the reminder of the historical memory of oppression in Egypt and God's deliverance. Although the comfort and the power of land remains a temptation to forget God and become oppressors, the land comes with the Torah—thus the exhortation to remember God and care for the weak and vulnerable in the community. Israel's relationship with God thus includes in its web not only the *gērim*, but the land itself, and the most vulnerable people in the land. The charge to remember is actually a spur to remember the nature and history of the relationship of the people of God *with* God.

The Israelites are not guaranteed permanent possession of the land. The consequence of forgetting the nature of these relationships and their corresponding responsibilities is the loss of the land itself. The theology of Deuteronomy, written during the Babylonian exile, is insistent in its reminder that Israel will lose the land if it forgets the Torah. Therefore, the barrier that divides the Israelites from the *gērim* is porous. The Israelites had been *gērim* in their past, and, as the Deuteronomist knew well, they would be *gērim* again in their future. As Frank Crüsemann points out, the very future of the Israelites depends on how they treat the strangers in their midst.[34] The prophets of the exile, Jeremiah and Ezekiel, specifically warn against oppressing the widow, orphan, and stranger (Jer. 7:6; 22:3; Ezek. 22:7). The identity of the Israelites as *gērim* in Egypt and in Babylon suggests a relationship with the *gērim* in Israel that resists the easy division into "us" and "the other," which characterized the pharaoh's policy toward the Israelites.

The complicated relationship of the Israelites, the God who loves strangers, and the land provides a direction for an account of justice that can respond to the complicated relationships between migrants and citizens today. One can imagine that the Israelites, who in their own history had been without their own land for a very long period, would have done everything

---

33. Brueggemann, *The Land*, 50–51.
34. Frank Crüsemann, "'You Know the Heart of a Stranger' (Exodus 23:9): A Recollection of Torah in the Face of New Nationalism and Xenophobia," in *Migrants and Refugees*, ed. Dietmar Mieth and Lisa Sowle Cahill (Maryknoll, NY: Orbis, 1993), 106–7.

they could to ensure that the land remained theirs. Given their history, Israel would have been tempted to be extremely suspicious of the *gērim* in their land, just as the pharaoh became suspicious of the Hebrews, who could one day take his people's land. Once maintaining possession of the land becomes more important that the covenant, strangers could come to be perceived as threats who could one day rise up against the Israelites. In other words, the "sacralization of the land"—making the land into an idol—could lead the Israelites to become Egyptians. Instead, the Torah reminds the Israelites of the right relationships among God, the Israelites, the land, and the *gērim*. God is the protector of the *gēr* and the giver of land. God reminds the Israelites that their possession of the land depends not on guarding their land against the *gērim*, but on loving them and ensuring justice for them.

These texts thus illustrate how "justice as fidelity to the demands of a relationship" operates in the legal materials on the *gēr*. The central relationships here—the Israelites' relationship with God and with the *gērim*—place demands on the Israelites, but these demands are only intelligible in the context of the narratives of the relationship of God with Israel and of Israel with Egypt. These narratives not only shape the Israelites' relationship with the *gērim* in their midst; they also shape the very identity of Israel. These narratives about relationship and identity shape narratives about moral values—justice, righteousness, and remembrance. The specific responsibilities that emerge from these narratives are outlined in the legal materials, but they are not fully intelligible without the narratives in which they are embedded.

The parallels to the relationships between migrants and citizens today should be obvious. The key temptation for citizens today is to subscribe to a false narrative, one that omits the origins of the relationships between migrants and citizens. Rather than perceiving migrants as those with whom there is a preexisting relationship, citizens forget this history and instead perceive migrants as a threat. In other words, injustice in relationships is a result of not having better narratives that include the ambiguities and tragedies of this history. Therefore, justice has something to do with having accurate narratives and being able to connect responsibilities to these narratives.

In Relation with Christ: The New Testament and the Stranger

This account of justice for the *gērim* mirrors biblical theologies of justice all over the Bible, in which justice is a relational category rather than an abstract moral ideal. While the New Testament texts were written in a different context than the legal materials of the Pentateuch were, they also base the right relationship with the stranger on a right relationship with God.

Unlike the Israelites before the Babylonian exile, the early Christian communities whose experiences birthed the Gospels and Epistles of the New Testament did not have a government of their own. Living under the Roman government, they could not determine their own political, social, and economic institutions. Thus, while there is no equivalent to the legal materials of the Hebrew Bible—which spell out specific policies for protecting strangers—in the New Testament, there is a correlative ethical imperative to extend hospitality to the stranger. This ethical imperative is also based on relationship, in this case the relationships in the Christian community in Jesus Christ.

In the New Testament, Jesus is portrayed both as a stranger himself and as a host to strangers. He is the literal outsider from Nazareth and is figuratively portrayed as a stranger: God in exile, rejected and killed by a "hostile, violent world."[35] Matthew 25 explicitly links the image of Jesus as a stranger with the moral imperative of hospitality: "I was a stranger and you welcomed me." Like the Hebrew Bible materials that place the *gēr* in the most-vulnerable triad, the Gospels identify the stranger as one of "the least of these" who reveal the face of Christ.

The synoptic Gospels also present Jesus as the host who welcomes, along with sinners and outcasts, even non-Jews into the kingdom of God, for example, the Syrophoenician woman, who asks Jesus to heal her daughter (Matt. 15:21–28; Mark 7:24–30); the centurion, who asks Jesus to heal his slave (Luke 7:1–10; Matt. 8:5–13); and the Samaritan woman at the well (John 4:1–30). Non-Jews also feature prominently in parables such as the Good Samaritan (Luke 10:25–37). According to Christine Pohl, this "dual-identity" of Jesus as both stranger and host provides the foundation for Christian hospitality.[36] Christians, as followers of Jesus, are called to be strangers themselves who are in some sense unwelcome in society; they are also called to be hosts to others who are made to feel unwelcome.

Like the Hebrew Bible laws that command protection for the *gērim*, the ethical mandates that command welcome and hospitality toward the stranger are based not on abstract moral laws but on a concrete relationship, in this case, on the concrete relationship between Jesus Christ and the church. The

35. Thomas W. Ogletree, *Hospitality to the Stranger: Dimensions of Moral Understanding* (Louisville: Westminster John Knox, 2003), 7.

36. Christine D. Pohl, "Hospitality from the Edge: The Significance of Marginality in the Practice of Welcome," *Annual for the Society of Christian Ethics* 15, no. 1 (2001): 126.

hungry, the thirsty, the stranger, the naked, the sick, and the prisoner of Matthew 25 all represent Christ, and by caring for the "least of these," the Christian community cares for Christ. The stranger cannot literally be a stranger, for the stranger is the literal personification of Jesus. Similarly, the stories of Jesus's interacting with and welcoming the foreigner bade the earliest Christian communities to welcome the non-Jew into their midst. This ethic of welcome comes from the relationship between the Christian community and the person of Christ—his example and his identity as a stranger.

The Epistles of the Pauline and pseudepigraphal Pauline corpora continue this theme of the relationship of the member and stranger in Christ. In view of the pluralistic world of Jews and Greeks, citizens and noncitizens of the Roman Empire, Paul affirms that one's identity as a Christian cannot be impeded by ethnic identity or cultural practices or citizenship because of the relationship between all members of the community. In this community of faith, familial and ethnic ties become irrelevant: "There is neither Jew nor Greek" (Gal. 3:28). Hence, the relationship of the various members of the body of Christ reconfigures political and ethnic divisions into a kind of unity. It is the relationship of various members of the body of Christ that reconfigures the relationship.

Conclusion: Justice in the Bible

The legal materials concerning the *gēr* can serve as a source for a Christian ethics of migration in at least two different ways. One way is to ask ourselves how the norms that minimize the vulnerability of the *gēr* could offer analogous protection in our own societies. But another way is to read these materials in the context of a larger account of justice in the Bible, one that draws on a central biblical narrative in order to establish that justice consists in living up to the demands of relationships. Instead of defining justice as a series of abstract norms, justice as fidelity to the demands of a relationship places norms in the context of particular narratives that demand particular responsibilities. This account of justice suggests that, at the very least, outsiders cannot be excluded from the sphere of our relationships simply because they are nonmembers. In addition, this account of justice suggests that responsibilities are grounded in narratives.

These biblical insights about justice can provide further direction for an ethics of migration. In the Hebrew Bible, the obligations of justice are most frequently put on those with the power and standing to enact right relationships between themselves and those considered "outside."[37] In other words, these right relationships must be "worked out in the reality of history, in which there are not subjects in general, but just and unjust subjects."[38] Thus, the particularity of persons—their social locations, their identities, and their histories—matters a great deal for justice and right relationships. The responsibilities we have in relationships are often commensurate with our power and standing; indeed, citizens may well have greater responsibilities to migrants than migrants have to citizens.

The materials from the Pentateuch, in particular, can model the reflection on relationships that are at the heart of justice, relationships that have their origins in particulars of history. Only via narrative can we understand what these relationships are and what responsibilities they give us. The Bible, however, cannot give us everything we need to develop a Christian ethics of migration that responds to migration-systems theory. The account of justice outlined here depends a great deal on a particular narrative: the narrative of the Exodus. This story functions as the metanarrative of the Hebrew Bible, offering a hermeneutical key to everything that comes after: the law, the prophets, and the writings. Citizens of contemporary liberal democracies do not share a religious metanarrative about their origins, but I have already suggested (in chapter 3) that it is neither possible nor desirable to have a master narrative. In addition, while the legal materials of the Pentateuch do the work of deriving specific responsibilities from narratives and relationships, the citizens and migrants of modern liberal democracies have no such manual that assigns specific responsibilities. The next chapter uses certain features of justice as *fidelity* to relationships as a model for justice as *responsibility* to relationships.

For Further Reading

Two books about the ongoing relevance of the Exodus story influenced my reading of it: Michael Walzer's *Exodus and Revolution* (New York: Basic Books, 1985) and Michael Goldberg's *Jews and Christians, Getting Our Stories Straight* (Philadelphia: Trinity Press International, 1991).

---

37. Pietro Bovani, *Re-establishing Justice: Legal Terms, Concepts, and Procedures in the Hebrew Bible*, trans. Michael J. Smith, Journal for the Study of the Old Testament Supplement Series 105 (Sheffield, UK: JSOT Press, 1994), 19.

38. Bovani, *Re-establishing Justice*, 19.

Bruce Birch's *Let Justice Roll Down: The Old Testament, Ethics, and Christian Life* (Louisville: Westminster John Knox, 1991) provides a useful account of how the Old Testament (or Hebrew Bible) can be used in Christian ethics.

For a fuller account of "justice as fidelity to the demands of a relationship," see the following two pieces by John Donahue: "Biblical Perspectives on Justice," in *The Faith That Does Justice*, edited by John Haughey (New York: Paulist Press, 1977), and "The Bible and Catholic Social Teaching," in *Modern Catholic Social Teaching: Commentaries and Interpretations*, edited by Kenneth R. Himes et al. (Washington, DC: Georgetown University Press, 2005).

CHAPTER 6

Justice as Responsibility to Relationships

Migration presents ethical questions that many Christian ethics theorists do not adequately answer: What responsibilities do citizens have toward migrants and potential migrants? What is the basis of these responsibilities? In the public sphere, our answers to these questions are rooted in false narratives about the relationships between migrants and citizens. In order to answer the central questions of migration, we need not only new narratives but a new account of justice that allocates responsibilities rather than merely human rights. I call this account *justice as responsibility to relationships*.

While many Christian perspectives of the ethics of migration have drawn extensively on human rights and other kinds of universal commitments, particular attachments and obligations have been neglected. *Justice as responsibility* is my attempt to navigate between universal and particular commitments, maintaining the importance of both universal human rights and particular responsibilities. Justice as responsibility sets both universal and particular commitments in thick contexts, which include unchosen relationships and institutions. This attention to particularity is especially important in the context of global justice. As we have seen in chapter 4, justice in the domestic sphere often implicitly draws on social contracts and other concepts that in some way delimit our responsibilities to one another. In discussions about global justice, however, there are few institutions that spell out our responsibilities to distant others. Migrants and potential migrants thus often fall outside the normal distributions of responsibility; and hence the particularity and specificity of understanding justice as responsibility to relationships is critical in the context of globalization.

We have explored how the biblical definition of justice as "fidelity to the demands of a relationship" is manifested in the biblical materials dealing with the *gēr*. This biblical perspective on justice, which roots specific laws in narratives about relationships and identity, is the basis for the account of justice that I develop in this final chapter—that is, justice as responsibility to relationships (hereafter, justice as responsibility), which has three characteristics. First, justice as responsibility takes as its starting point the messy, complicated, and ambiguous relationships in which we find ourselves. Rather than seeing these unchosen relationships as obstacles to the realization of justice, justice as responsibility takes as its task the discernment of responsibilities in the midst of these historical relationships and the context of our own injuries and our fallibility.

The second characteristic is that justice as responsibility sees responsibility itself as a social good, which, like other social goods, is produced and distributed in communal life. In other words, like the theories of justice I analyzed in chapter 4, justice as responsibility considers the normative distribution of social goods a central concern of justice. However, unlike these other theories, justice as responsibility sees responsibility itself as a "background" social good that directs the distribution of other social goods—such as health care and education.

In other words, responsibilities are not distributed solely by means of a biological or natural order, though many responsibilities are the byproduct of our embodiment and vulnerability. Rather, responsibilities are distributed by means of social narratives that map responsibilities onto various kinds of relationships. However, these narratives do not always tell the right stories about what I call reality. Instead, narratives can map responsibilities inaccurately or unjustly. The just allocation of responsibility is possible only when we ask existing social narratives about how true they are to reality. Where narratives are false, they must be replaced by better narratives. Justice as responsibility incorporates the option for the poor not as a universal directive to care for the poor but as a reminder that those whose voices are ignored or forgotten are those whose perspectives are most often left out of social narratives.

Justice as responsibility eschews neither the option for the poor nor universal human rights. However, unlike theories of human rights that detail thick accounts of positive rights without specifying who has the duty to provide for these rights, justice as responsibility locates the responsibility to provide these positive goods in the specific relationships that bind people to each other.[1]

---

1. Following Iris Marion Young, I distinguish responsibilities from duties: duties are universal principles that bind all; responsibilities do not necessarily bind all. Determining what

The third characteristic of justice as responsibility is that it supplements, rather than supplants, structural theories of justice. That is to say, theories of justice are often divided into classical theories of justice that treat justice as a personal virtue, and into contemporary theories of justice that emphasize justice as a characteristic of the "basic structure of society."[2] Relational accounts of justice often discard or neglect structural dimensions of justice—and vice versa.[3] In emphasizing a relational account of justice, justice as responsibility does not overlook or neglect structural dimensions of justice; rather, justice as responsibility intersects with structural justice. As we have seen in chapter 3, structural injustice conditions and entrenches false narratives that obscure our responsibilities to others. In other words, narratives themselves are often the result of complex social structural processes in which we all participate. Just social structures produce and reproduce accurate narratives; unjust social structures produce and reproduce unjust narratives.

The Ethics of Responsibility

The ethics of responsibility, as a framework for justice as responsibility to relationships, helps us determine not the what (which is satisfactorily answered by Christian and other perspectives on human rights) but the who: Who must be responsible for protecting these rights of migrants? The ethics of responsibility is a relatively new way of looking at moral questions: it is at once distinct from virtue ethics, deontological and teleological forms of moral theories, and, at its most basic, focuses on the responsibilities that moral agents have to one another and to nonhuman creation.[4] The roots of responsibility ethics lie deep within the Christian tradition: in the Hebrew

---

responsibilities one possesses and how to discharge those responsibilities leaves more to judgment (Young, *Responsibility for Justice*, 143).

2. Young, *Responsibility for Justice*, chap. 2.

3. O'Neill, *Towards Justice and Virtue*, chap. 1.

4. Walker, *Moral Understandings*, 7; see also William Schweiker, "Responsibility and Moral Realities," *Studies in Christian Ethics* 22, no. 4 (2009): 480. The philosophical and theological literature on responsibility is extensive. The present discussion leaves aside many of the nuances within this literature in order to focus on the nature of human agency and the context of moral action. For a fuller account of the history of the concept of responsibility in philosophy and theology, see William Schweiker, *Responsibility and Christian Ethics*, New Studies in Christian Ethics (Cambridge: Cambridge University Press, 1995), chaps. 3–4; see also Albino Barrera, *Market Complicity and Christian Ethics* (Cambridge: Cambridge University Press, 2011), chap. 9.

Bible and the New Testament Gospels, and in the documentary tradition of Catholic social thought.[5] The idea of responsibility is a key element in the thought of Saint Thomas Aquinas, who posits that moral agents have the responsibility to contribute to the common good as the proximate end of society.[6] However, as William Schweiker describes it, the ethics of responsibility refers to much more than the rather obvious point that, as moral agents, we are responsible for harms that we cause; it is also more broadly concerned with the context and possibilities of moral action. The ethics of responsibility makes two contributions to justice as responsibility.

The first contribution is that justice as responsibility adopts the realism of the ethics of responsibility. Rather than understanding the complex, interlocking processes of structural sin that form migration systems as either an aberration of or an obstacle to the realization of justice, the ethics of responsibility understands these political, social, and historical systems as a starting point. They are part of the moral context in which we must make decisions about how to act. The second contribution that an ethics of responsibility makes to justice as responsibility is that such an ethics can help us understand the role of narratives in allocating responsibilities.

Realism

Justice as responsibility to relationships adopts the realism of responsibility ethics in starting from the reality that persons can and do act across national borders. In contrast to John Rawls's sporadic treatment of migration, justice as responsibility cannot treat migration as a rare exception to a bounded

---

5. Barrera, *Market Complicity and Christian Ethics*, 243–55.

6. Schweiker, "Responsibility and Moral Realities," 484; see also Barrera, *Market Complicity and Christian Ethics*, 242–43. Though both Schweiker and Barrera insist that two major strands of Catholic social ethics—the thought of Thomas Aquinas and the documentary tradition of magisterial Catholic social thought—are compatible with the ethics of responsibility, Catholic social ethics has to date focused on the needs and rights of vulnerable people without specifying who has either the obligation or the responsibility to provide for them. Pope Francis's environmental encyclical, *Laudato si'*, may represent a departure from this trend, since the encyclical presents a multilayered account of responsibility for the care of the earth. Individuals, governments, and "cooperatives" all have different responsibilities to tackle in both the ideological and material causes of climate change. Though Pope Francis does not delve deeply into sorting out these different responsibilities, we can imagine that these varying responsibilities come from the capacity of different agents to effect different kinds of change. However, sustained reflection on the responsibilities of moral agents is lacking in the field of Catholic social ethics.

world; it is a feature of the complex patterns of interaction that make up the moral world of agents. And while Martha Nussbaum argues that all persons have the obligation to protect the capabilities of all other persons, responsibility ethics would ask more difficult questions than she does about the actual capacities of specific persons to shoulder these responsibilities.[7] Those with less power have fewer responsibilities because their actual capacity to act is reduced by their circumstances.[8] Citizens who are in positions of power may have greater responsibilities to migrants than vulnerable migrants have to citizens, as others have argued. But citizens may also have conflicting responsibilities to different groups of migrants that might conflict with each other. These insights also work in the opposite direction: some migrants might have responsibilities to their own families or communities that conflict with their responsibilities to citizens; other migrants, however, might have greater responsibilities to citizens. Finally, unlike O'Neill's deontological ethics, the ethics of responsibility speaks of responsibilities rather than obligations. Unlike obligations, which in Kant's account are universal principles that bind all persons, responsibilities are sensitive to variations in community, in relationships, and to the actual human capacities to act. Therefore, justice as responsibility to relationship acknowledges that citizens might have different responsibilities to different groups of citizens and migrants.

In addition to contributing a contextual realism to justice as responsibility, the ethics of migration also contributes a moral realism. William Schweiker says: "It insists on the realities that limit human action and aspiration, and it is unbendingly honest about threats of self-deception" (487). Schweiker thus draws on the work of H. Richard Niebuhr to present people as situated within "patterns and processes of interdependence [that require] attention to the impact and consequences on the parts of the whole" (483). James Gustafson has called this a "common-sense ontology," in which the "patterns of responsiveness, the feedback loops that define the interactions among and between forces and their environments, create the conditions for present life that form the moral space of human life" (quoted at 485). Schweiker's account

---

7. Nussbaum does acknowledge that those who are themselves struggling for their flourishing should not bear primary responsibility for solving the problems of the world's most disadvantaged; however, it is not clear how this uneven distribution of responsibilities squares with her insistence that universal responsibilities protect the capabilities (Nussbaum, *Frontiers of Justice*, 321).

8. Schweiker, "Responsibility and Moral Realities," 487. Hereafter, page references to this essay appear in parentheses within the text.

of this moral space before God echoes Margaret Farley's account of agency-in-relation, in which moral agents act on and are acted on by the vast web of relationships in which they exist from birth. Therefore, the moral context of an ethics of migration, like the context of all ethical judgment, is fraught, marked with sinful social-structural processes, the wounds of history, and conflicting and competing loyalties. Neglecting this context can "too easily blind one to the conflicting powers and realities that form the environment of conduct" (491). That is, moral norms, whatever they are, are not necessarily easy to apply. Within the unjust social-structural processes, it is not always clear what moral responsibilities we have and how we should meet them.

Rather than understanding the complex, interlocking processes of structural sin that cause migration to be an obstacle to the realization of justice, the ethics of responsibility understands these political, social, and historical systems as part of the moral context in which we must fulfill our responsibilities. The context in which citizens and their governments make judgments about their responsibilities to migrants is a deeply complex context of historical wrongs, unchosen relationships, and conflicting claims by both needy and vulnerable migrants and citizens. The moral context of global justice is characterized by the very absence of social contracts that in the domestic society clarify our responsibilities to one another. And yet the acknowledgment of these complex histories and their moral confusion is crucial for any ethics of migration. Awareness of this fraught context prevents an ethics of migration from asserting uncomplicated universals about the rights of migrants without engaging the difficult realities that surround actually meeting the rights of migrants.

Yet these complications do not excuse us from our responsibilities. The ethics of responsibility is attentive to a central irony about moral action: To be a person is to be a moral agent, "that being . . . who can 'take responsibility' for actions and relations" (486). However, even this distinctively human capacity for moral agency is not without limitation. As agents, we are not only temporally and spatially limited; our judgment and our power are also limited (487). We harm without intent, and we cannot always rectify our wrongs. These limitations are also a part of the ethics of responsibility. (I will return to this last point later in this chapter.)

The ethics of responsibility does not limit itself to this focus on the context, possibilities, and limitations of moral actions; Schweiker insists that such an ethics requires moral norms to guide it (491). The ethics of responsibility thus can operate in tandem with, and in fact requires, other moral norms. Whereas Schweiker proposes the norm of "respecting and enhancing

119

the integrity of life" as a nonanthropocentric norm that includes human responsibility to all of creation, I am more satisfied with traditional accounts of positive and negative rights and/or Nussbaum's capabilities approach. In a framework of responsibility ethics, these approaches need not be simplistic. If the flaw of human rights and capability approaches is that they do not pay attention to the complicated endeavor of assigning responsibilities, nor to the reality of complicated histories of relationships, the ethics of responsibility can demand that such approaches attend to these contexts. Therefore, an ethics of migration need not stop at insisting that migrants possess the spectrum of human rights. Responsibility ethics requires sorting out who has the responsibility to provide for the rights of migrants and to determine on what basis responsibilities are to be allocated.

Narrative

This brings us to the second contribution that an ethics of responsibility can make to an ethics of migration: an ethics of responsibility can help us understand that responsibilities are allocated through complex social narratives. This ethic can also show us that one task of justice is to interrogate and, where necessary, to reframe these narratives.

It is thought to be a commonsense moral insight that people have general responsibility to strangers, but they have special responsibilities to those who are in close relationships with them.[9] General responsibilities include the principles of benevolence (the obligation to do good) and non-maleficence (the obligation not to harm another) and the duty to be of mutual aid (the responsibility to help others in need). In close relationships, however, common sense tells us that responsibilities are much stronger than the general imperatives of benevolence, non-maleficence, and mutual aid. Parents have specific responsibilities to provide for and care for their own children that they do not have to the children of others. Likewise, adult children have responsibilities to their elderly parents that they do not have toward the elderly in general. Much work on responsibilities and global justice boils down to sorting through how these special responsibilities and general responsibilities relate to each other.[10]

9. Samuel Scheffler, *Boundaries and Allegiances: Problems of Justice and Responsibility in Liberal Thought* (Oxford: Oxford University Press, 2001), 36.
10. See, e.g., Goodin, "What Is So Special about Our Fellow Countrymen?"; see also Scheffler, *Boundaries and Allegiances*, 36.

But sorting through who has responsibilities—to whom and for what—is not as straightforward as simply reading special responsibilities from special relationships. Responsibilities are, in fact, allocated by way of complex narratives about our relationships, and these play out in a variety of specific social practices.[11] These narratives are often invisible to us because they are often a part of the moral reality that we take for granted, which is true within both the domestic society and the global society. For example, even the commonsense claim that parents have the responsibility to provide for, emotionally nurture, and physically care for their own dependent children plays out in these culturally bound narratives and social practices. Margaret Urban Walker points to the multiple ways in which parental responsibilities are grounded in specific social practices rather than biological needs alone:

> A society such as ours in the contemporary U.S. has selected a practice of assigning responsibility for basic child maintenance and supervision primarily, and nearly exclusively, to adult members of some (one) nuclear family to which the child "belongs." Public participation and support for these functions in children's early years, essentially ancillary or remedial in this system, are meager, unusually punitive, and often stigmatized.[12]

In other words, while it is tempting to adopt the simple, commonsense notion that certain kinds of relationships lead to certain kinds of responsibilities, Walker shows how even such seemingly obvious connections are mediated through social practices that allocate responsibilities. However, these social practices are not impervious to examination, critique, and, ultimately, transformation.[13]

How, then, do we go about assessing our own practices of responsibility and changing them, if change is required? Despite the fact that our own norms concerning the distribution of responsibility for childcare seem so obvious to us that they become invisible, these norms are in fact connected to social narratives that underlie these practices. The traditionalist view of parental responsibility rests on social narratives about who mothers and fathers are supposed be as providers and nurturers. In the traditionalist narrative, the ideal father thus provides a sufficient income so that the mother of his children can stay home. The ideal traditionalist mother's

11. Walker, *Moral Understandings*, chap. 4.
12. Walker, *Moral Understandings*, 89.
13. Walker, *Moral Understandings*, 104–5.

chief responsibility is to care for the physical and emotional needs of her children and provide for their well-being. The implication of distributing responsibilities among members of the nuclear family in that way is that families who require assistance from others outside the family, such as the state, are failing in their gendered responsibilities. Perhaps a father cannot find a job that provides for his family. Perhaps the mother chooses a partner for herself and a father for her children who is not responsible enough to stick around. The traditionalist narrative, which influences even those who claim they reject it, stigmatizes the inability of parents to provide for their children as failures of personal responsibility. That is why, as Walker describes it, public assistance is meager, and reliance on that assistance is stigmatized.

While narratives are often so obvious to us as to be invisible, they can in fact be more or less faithful to what I will call the fullness of reality. Narratives that are more faithful to reality reflect more accurately the ambiguities of history: who people are and who they want to be, the complexities of our relationships, the givenness of our biological needs and wants, and so forth. In this case, feminist activists and scholars have uncovered the problem with these dominant narratives of ideal motherhood and fatherhood: they do not tell the full stories of either the identities of women and men or of the social realities of parenthood in our society. The idea that women have an essential nature that is ideally suited to full-time caregiving has long been rejected by feminist thinkers. Furthermore, the social and economic realities of work in twenty-first-century North America are that fewer and fewer families are able to survive on one income. The identity of "ideal father" as sole provider for his family is unattainable for most men. If such narratives were changed to reflect these realities, we might come to quite different conclusions about how the responsibilities for childcare should be allocated in our society.

Just as the allocation of responsibilities based on relationships are neither simple nor straightforward, the allocation of responsibilities based on the narratives that we have about our relationships are likewise complex. As universal human rights can be protected by a variety of different institutional arrangements, so responsibilities can be allocated in various ways, some of them more or less just. Walker disposes of the distinction between special and general responsibilities by placing all responsibilities within thick "geographies of responsibilities." In effect, there are no general responsibilities. "We are all of us 'special' in some respects. We are not all responsible for the same things, in the same ways, at the same costs, or with similar exposure to demand or blame by the same judges."[14] Similarly, there is no metric of general and special responsibilities that can cover the distinction between citizens and migrants. In the current condition of the world, we are already tangled up with one another in specific, special relationships.

This second contribution of an ethics of responsibility to an ethics of migration thus shows that responsibilities are allocated by complex narratives about relationships. Although there is no simple way to sort through what our responsibilities are, this very complexity is an advantage of the ethics of responsibility. The ethics of responsibility suggests that a central task of an ethics of migration must be to examine, to critique, and to revise the narratives that we have about our relationships.

Justice as Responsibility to Relationships

This task of naming our narratives concerning our responsibilities and critically assessing them is, in fact, a task of justice. Many contemporary theories of justice concern the normative distribution of social goods: who should get what. Other theories of justice, following John Rawls's *A Theory of Justice*, often address what Rawls terms the "basic structure of society": the background social, economic, and political institutions that ultimately ground the distribution of both the benefits and the burdens that result from life in society.[15] If we look at theories of justice through the lens of responsibility ethics, we see that all of these accounts of justice operate in tandem with implicit accounts of responsibility. As we have seen, the theory of the social contract, the basis of Rawls's account of justice, assumes that citizens have responsibilities to one another based on their common membership in a political community, responsibilities that they do not have to outsiders. While Rawls does not state this explicitly, Michael Walzer does: "Membership is important because of what the members of a political community owe to one another and to no one else, or to no one else in the same degree."[16]

Theories of justice not only implicitly assume an account of responsibilities; they also assert norms about the production and distribution of responsibilities. In other words, responsibilities are themselves a kind of social

14. Walker, *Moral Understandings*, 99.
15. Rawls, *A Theory of Justice*, 7.
16. Walzer, *Spheres of Justice*, 64.

good or burden that gets produced and distributed by societies. Some responsibilities are biological givens that must be distributed: the need to care for children, the disabled, and the elderly; the need to dispose of waste and clean up after ourselves; the need to provide and prepare food for ourselves and others. Other kinds of responsibilities come from our social life together and are in some sense socially produced: the responsibility of political leadership and decision-making; the responsibility of protecting society from criminals and protecting criminals from injustice, and so on. While some of these responsibilities may be considered social burdens—for example, the responsibility of disposing of waste—others may be considered social goods, for example, the responsibilities associated with political leadership. Other responsibilities might be both benefit and burden, for example, providing care for dependent children. While these responsibilities are biological and social givens, the specific forms that these responsibilities take and how they are distributed may vary dramatically from one society to another.

Margaret Walker's analysis of the responsibilities of parents points to the ways our allocation of responsibility are institutionalized in our social structures.[17] Because other members of society are understood not to have many responsibilities for the survival and education of other people's children, contemporary US society lacks a strong welfare system, one that would include provisions for paid maternity and paternity leave and other structural supports for parents. Many political philosophers and theologians would say that this method of distributing responsibilities is unjust on many grounds. For example, it leaves poor children facing a lifetime of the consequences of poverty. Furthermore, women face unequal burdens in caring for children. A just basic structure depends on an accurate account of the responsibilities that we have to one another; an unjust basic structure reproduces itself in part by reproducing an unjust account and distribution of responsibilities.

Justice as responsibility to relationships suggests that justice concerns not only who gets what; it also concerns the relationships and responsibilities that connect us to each other. This is not to say that the contemporary accounts of justice that emphasize normative distribution, or the justness of background institutions, are wrong or irrelevant. In fact, just background institutions are crucial for the just distribution of goods. However, an evaluation of responsibility is crucial for any account of justice, since responsibility is one of the social goods (or burdens) that gets produced and distributed. Moreover, social structures do not arise out of nowhere; they are

17. Walker, *Moral Understandings*, 89.

themselves, in part, the products of the accounts of our responsibilities to one another. Relationships are often institutionalized in social structures. Reforming unjust social structures often involves both a critical look at the current distribution of responsibilities and the ability to develop new, more accurate accounts of our responsibilities to each other.

When we turn to questions of transnational justice, the question of responsibilities becomes even more crucial, because there is no social contract that lays out the basic responsibilities that people have to one another. Not only is there no social contract that spans societies; the relationships themselves that cross borders are often hidden from us. Therefore, the South American farmers who grow coffee for the North American market are in a sense hidden from the consumers, and we are unlikely to know their living and working conditions. The task of transnational justice must not be merely to examine and reform inconsistent or inaccurate narratives. In many cases, there may be no narrative at all about these distant others. Without knowing the actual peoples—and without understanding our relationships with them and the responsibilities that might accompany these relationships—we cannot know how to treat them justly.

Justice as responsibility, therefore, requires an understanding of the particularities of the relationships binding peoples across borders. It may require us to construct narratives where there are none and to critically examine the narratives we do have. It requires reflection on how we should proceed in the absence of narrative. The full range of questions surrounding transnational justice is beyond the scope of this book, but the question of citizens' responsibilities toward migrants is a part of the topic of transnational justice.

In some ways, the relationships between citizens and migrants—or citizens and potential migrants—are not like the relationships between consumers and hidden farm or factory workers. Narratives about migrants are almost always at work because migrants live among citizens, and they figure prominently in the media and in political discourse. Even potential migrants are not altogether hidden from citizens. Central Americans who ride "the beast" through Mexico en route to the United States, or Africans who cross the Mediterranean en route to continental Europe, are the subject of policy discussions and debates in the developed world. In these cases, what is hidden from view is not the relationship itself but the narratives that underlie our discussions. As we have seen, the narrative about the relationships between citizens and migrants is too often the narrative expressed by the view of neoclassical migration theory: citizens are the generous hosts to needy and distant strangers. I have tried to show in this book why that narrative is false, and I have suggested that there are other narratives that more accurately describe the relationship between citizens and migrants. Thus the question is: How do these alternate narratives result in a different understanding of responsibilities toward migrants?

A partial answer to this question is suggested by Christian ethicist Christopher Steck, who, in a 2004 article, first retells the story of US-Mexico undocumented migration in terms of migration-systems theory and then offers the following corrective to the US policy on citizenship and naturalization:

> My claim here is not one of economic justice, or at least not justice narrowly understood. It is not simply that U.S. business or the U.S. itself owes the Mexican people something for past business practices using Mexican labor—that may be true, but it is not my point. My interest is rather that the U.S. acknowledge the history of this relationship and how deeply it continues to affect the lives of millions of Mexicans and that such an acknowledgment can and should lead to efforts to strengthen those bonds and, where necessary, heal them of their harmful effects.[18]

In this essay Steck points to the fact that US policy reforms are dependent on an accurate narrative of Americans' relationship with Mexicans, a relationship that is informed by an accurate reading of history and its connection to the present. And Steck's insight here would fall squarely within an account of justice as responsibility to relationships that I am seeking to articulate in this book.

Steck's analysis of the relationship between citizens of the United States and Mexican migrants indicates a few other features of the role of narratives in allocating responsibilities. The first feature is that there is no one totalizing narrative that determines the responsibilities of all citizens to all migrants. Steck's narrative is specific: it is based on details that are unique to the US relationship with Mexico. The details of each relationship matter to the responsibilities that emerge from them. Thus, the responsibilities of US citizens to Mexicans may well differ from the responsibilities of US citizens to Central Americans fleeing gang violence, which may, in turn, differ

18. Christopher Steck, "Solidarity, Citizenship, and Globalization: Developing a New Framework for Theological Reflections on U.S.-Mexico Immigration," *Journal of Peace and Justice Studies* 14, no. 2 (2004): 171.

from the responsibilities of US citizens to Iraqi refugees fleeing the violence of wars. Once we change the setting of the stories, the details change once again—and so would the narratives.

The second feature that emerges from Steck's analysis is that narratives must be what I call "faithful to reality." In other words, Steck rejects false, incomplete, or inadequate narratives about the relationship between the United States and Mexico and attempts to replace them with a narrative that better accounts for what this relationship really is. The retelling of the narratives of relationship between certain groups of citizens and migrants (in chapter 3 above) has the same purpose. In using the word "reality," I am not speaking exclusively of historical accuracy, though that may be a part of it; reality includes the full picture of what is going on in all of its historical, social, economic, and moral complexity. In some cases, historical accuracy may not impact whether the narrative is faithful to reality. For example, the role of the Exodus narrative in the Hebrew Bible was to inspire the Israelites to recall the moral truth of their relationship with God. In the case of the Exodus, the "reality" of the narrative cannot be ascertained by any verification of its historicity, because the social practices that derive from the Exodus narrative—such as the norms for the resident alien in ancient Israel—are based on theological rather than historical claims about the relationship between God and Israel.

However, when we speak of the relationship between migrants and citizens today, we cannot avoid historicity. This is partly because certain historical relationships lead to migration and partly because the facticity of what happened and is happening is a part of how we, as moderns, understand our moral world. Therefore, the retelling of narratives highlights the overlooked connection between historical events and migration patterns, as described by migration theorists. Despite the importance of history, the fullness of reality cannot be completely captured by a recitation of historical events. The narratives use not only the tools of history but those of policy, sociology, and philosophy. The facts of history must be "read" through these other disciplines, which illuminate how these narratives matter and how they distribute responsibility.

In addition, any narrative necessarily includes some details and omits others; some facts, perspectives, and insights are emphasized while others may be de-emphasized or omitted entirely. A list of every historical fact, policy detail, and sociological insight is not a narrative; rather, it is a list of facts. For a narrative to make sense as a story, the kind of story that can challenge understandings and suggest new distributions of responsibility, it must be a partial narrative. Narratives must strive for fidelity to reality, though they will ultimately fall short. We must hence be humble about our narratives and aware of their limitations. We must also be open to revising our narratives.

No one narrative can capture the fullness of reality. In the words of novelist Chimamanda Ngozi Adichie, there is a "danger of a single story" because it purports to be the only story, mirroring the perspective of the dominant group and entrenching unjust practices.[19] For this reason, Iris Marion Young writes that "the politics of historical narrative should make room for plural stories." In other words, providing space for a plurality of narratives ensures that no one narrative becomes dominant. In advocating for a plurality of narratives, Young is not envisioning that different groups will tell different stories in isolation from one another. She envisions a public process in which narratives are reconstituted by means of "political contest, debate, and the acknowledgment of diverse perspectives on the stories and the stakes."[20] While narratives are not ever able to perfectly capture reality, the sharing of our narratives in the public sphere leads to narratives that are more faithful to reality.

Discerning which narratives are more faithful to reality, however, involves not just acknowledging the plurality of narratives. Dominant narratives often obscure the experiences and insights of those on the margins of society, including migrants, precisely because the structures of sin that benefit the powerful often obscure the narratives of those who are exploited. It is not enough to make room for a plurality of narratives. We must pay special attention to the narratives that represent the voices and experiences of those who have traditionally been ignored or marginalized, as well as to the narratives of the "victims of history"—those who are no longer here to tell their tale.[21] This is not because these overlooked or forgotten narratives are automatically more faithful to reality; they may or may not be. But those narratives can challenge the *mainstream* narrative and enable us to look for what Margaret Urban Walker calls "inconsistencies, lies, and embarrassments."[22] The narratives of marginalized voices can also help expose the places where the dominant narrative merely reproduces the interests of the powerful. Therefore, incorporating the perspectives of the powerless and forgotten helps narratives become more faithful to reality.

19. Chimamanda Ngozi Adichie, "The Danger of a Single Story," TED: Ideas Worth Sharing, October 2009, https://www.ted.com/talks/chimamanda_adichie_the_danger_of_a_single_story/transcript?language=en.

20. Young, *Responsibility for Justice*, 182.

21. This phrase comes from the work of Johann Baptist Metz.

22. Walker, *Moral Understandings*, 219.

In this way, justice as responsibility to relationships incorporates the theological principle of the preferential option for the poor. However, here the option for the poor is not a general mandate prioritizing the poor in one's circle of responsibilities; instead, in justice as responsibility, the option for the poor functions as a way to include overlooked, suppressed, and forgotten narratives into the public discussion and debate. Such narratives are crucial if narratives are to capture reality more accurately. Because narratives will always fall short of completely capturing reality, we will need to continuously reexamine narratives, to subject them to the examination of the other disciplines, and to incorporate in them the perspectives of those who are ignored.

In order to challenge the dominant narrative that migrants are the needy and poor beneficiaries of the generosity of citizens, we must tell new stories by incorporating the socially and politically ignored histories of colonialism, guest-worker programs, and foreign investment. In exposing the connections between these ignored or forgotten histories and the migration systems they generate, we can tell a new story about migration, a story about the denial of histories and the turning away from the responsibilities that these histories generate.

Mapping Responsibilities to Migrants

So far I have argued that justice requires responsibility to relationships, that the content of these responsibilities is in some ways linked to the specifics of a relationship, and that sorting through responsibilities is a complex task that requires narratives about the relationships between citizens and migrants. Determining what specific responsibilities come from what relationships is a complicated and fraught endeavor, tied to the historical particularities of each relationship. But in what follows I will reflect more generally on what kinds of relationships between migrants and citizens lead to what kinds of responsibility. I do not intend to create a universal metric that can be used to determine in what circumstances political communities have what responsibilities for which migrants. As Walker's discussion of narrative shows us, the connection between relationships and responsibilities always runs through complex social narratives. Interrogating these narratives and replacing them with better narratives requires paying attention to the specifics of relationships in a way that cannot be reduced to universal principles. Instead, I wish to demonstrate how citizens can think about their relationships to various migrants in a way that illuminates rather than obscures their responsibilities. I examine four kinds of relationships: (1) the relationships between undocumented workers and citizens; (2) the relationships between the citizens of former colonial powers and migrants from former colonies; (3) the relationships among the citizens of countries that had guest-worker programs and the descendants of those guest workers; and (4) the relationships between the citizens of countries that benefit from free trade arrangements and migrants from countries that do not.

Undocumented Workers and Citizens

While all who lack citizenship in the countries they reside in are vulnerable to some degree, undocumented migrants are particularly vulnerable. Unlike legal migrants, undocumented migrants are in the territory not at the whim of the host country; they are there in defiance of it. And yet, the relationship between these two parties is much more complex than the simple and false narratives of citizens as makers of law and undocumented migrants as breakers of law. Kristin Heyer draws attention to the ways in which citizens of the United States actively participate in unjust economic structures that exploit and dehumanize undocumented migrants.[23] These migrants live alongside citizens, performing unpleasant but necessary labor. Citizens benefit from the cheap labor of those who mow lawns, care for children and elders, build homes, and pick the vegetables and fruits that end up on the dinner tables of citizens. Simply by eating dinner, citizens participate in the structures of sin that take advantage of undocumented migrants. This participation does not require any ill will. In fact, opting out of this participation would require almost superhuman amounts of attention, time, and money simply because the structures have become so much a part of the way citizens live their lives. Even if it were possible to opt out, our own participation is often obscured from us in ways that would make it difficult to know whether opting out is necessary or possible. We don't know who picks our tomatoes. Even if we shop at farmers' markets, we don't know whether the farmer employs undocumented migrants, or even if she does not, how well or poorly she pays her workers. Responsibilities to undocumented migrants come from this unwitting participation in labor markets that benefit from the labor of these migrants.

23. Heyer, *Kinship across Borders*, 46–47.

In many Western democracies, undocumented migrants provide this kind of labor. This account of responsibilities suggests that citizens have the responsibility to ensure that the migrants who provide needed services for them are included in the distribution of social benefits. Instead, undocumented migrants are "locked into an inferior position that is also an anomalous position . . . outcasts in a society that has no caste norms, metics in a society where metics have no comprehensible, protected and dignified place." They are in situations of tyranny, ruled by citizens who in many cases look just like they do.[24]

While many left-wing proposals argue that undocumented migrants should be offered amnesty from deportation and a "path to citizenship," justice as responsibility eschews the language of both amnesty and forgiveness.[25] These terms focus on the fact that undocumented migrants crossed a border in violation of civil law. However, a counternarrative focuses on the economic structures that drive migration and citizens' participation in these structures. This counternarrative emphasizes the contributions of undocumented migrants to the economies of their host countries and argues that these contributions should be justly remunerated. Citizens thus have responsibilities to undocumented migrants that are based not solely on a humanitarian interest in the welfare of migrants but also on this narrative of participation.

Understanding the relationship between citizens and migrants by taking a snapshot of the present distribution of benefits and burdens only tells part of the story of the relationship between citizens and migrants. As we have seen, that relationship is often rooted in the relationships of the past, sometimes the distant past. More often than not, citizens are living with the consequences of the actions of their predecessors. Their participation is itself conditioned by these relationships. Limiting considerations of responsibility to participation in social structures misses the responsibilities that these historical relationships might bring. For example, in the account I have just presented, the responsibilities of citizens are rooted in the participation of citizens in exploitative labor markets. However, as we have seen, such practices are often layered over histories that long preceded the current segmentation of the labor market. How do these histories figure into responsibilities?

---

24. Walzer, *Spheres of Justice*, 59. Here Walzer is speaking of the position of guest workers and their descendants who lived in European cities without the security of citizenship. However, I think that his description applies to undocumented migrants today.

25. See, e.g., Ahn, *Religious Ethics and Migration*, chaps. 1–2.

While few ethicists of migration have addressed these questions directly, the question of what is owed as a result of past wrongs has been much discussed by political philosophers. Onora O'Neill rejects the idea that certain groups of people are owed restitution for past injustices, arguing that it is nearly impossible to trace a causal link between current-day poverty and specific agents of the past. Given that the perpetrators are dead, how can we make judgments about who owes what to whom among their descendants?[26] Iris Marion Young offers a similar caution against "backward-looking" models of responsibility that seek to assign liability for harm.[27] Even if we could assign responsibility for harm, given the magnitude of the crimes and the losses of the victims, how is reparation even possible?[28] I agree that attempting to assign responsibility for crimes against humanity committed decades or centuries ago is a fruitless task. However, Young herself rejects a backward-looking liability model of responsibility and instead proposes a "forward-looking" social-connection model of responsibility. In other words, the past can give us responsibilities to the future that are not based on past harms but on our relational reality as participants in structural injustice.[29] In the case of these historical injustices, responsibilities derive not from participation alone but from these unchosen relationships that come from our past.

The first responsibility that emerges from historical injustices such as guest-worker programs and colonialism is simply to tell the narratives of these histories as harms. Guest-worker and colonial programs, as we have seen, both depended on racist ideologies, and both were to some degree exploitative. To the extent that these histories have been forgotten or whitewashed, they must be remembered. The academic discipline of history can assist with this remembrance, but the recovery of these narratives must not be confined to classes or seminars in universities; it must take place in the public sphere. The second responsibility that emerges from the past is that we might be called to reflect on our communal identities based on these narratives. Our communal identities, as Margaret Farley points out, cannot be entirely chosen by us. Thus the harms of colonialism and guest-worker programs must be deliberately and intentionally woven into the identities of the nations in question.

---

26. O'Neill, *Bounds of Justice*, 132.

27. Young, *Justice and the Politics of Difference*, 109.

28. Young, *Justice and the Politics of Difference*, 182.

29. Young, *Responsibility for Justice*, chap. 4.

The third responsibility we inherit from the past is that, wherever we find ourselves in exploitative relationships based on historical injustices, we transform those relationships into ones that can be characterized as right relationships. While the identities that are revealed by accurate narratives about past injustices may very well reveal ugliness, racism, and ethnocentrism, we are not trapped by these narratives. The paradox of the ethics of responsibility is that our actions are constrained by our histories and our context; yet we have the freedom—and the responsibility—to act within this context. Even though these relationships may be in some sense foisted on us, we bear the responsibility of shaping what these relationships will be in the future. Choosing our futures can never involve divorcing ourselves from our pasts, but must include becoming responsible for transforming the relationships of exploitation that we have inherited from the past.

Citizens, Colonial Migrants, and Their Descendants

Untangling the web of causality from colonial-era crimes to liability today is a hopeless task. As many have pointed out, colonial exploitation is only one factor that contributed to the poverty of what are developing countries today. Even if it were possible to trace a causal relationship between colonialism and poverty, it is unclear what responsibility the descendants of the colonists bear. But if we shift the focus from liability to relationship, the geography of responsibility becomes clearer.

The first responsibility is to recount the history of colonialism as a history of harm—enumerating all of its attendant abuses. The retelling of the narrative might involve considering how colonial-era figures are remembered in the public sphere. The second responsibility involves reflection on accompanying narratives of identity. Earlier I cited the novelist Zadie Smith's summation of British identity: "[T]here is no one more English than the Indian, no one more Indian than the English." Indeed, Indians and other former colonials speak the language of the host country; many of them were educated in schools that were modeled on schools of the host country; their food has often become the food of the host country. After all, curry is a British invention rather than a South Asian one.[30] Thus, in many ways, the colonial project succeeded in spreading British culture all

---

30. Uma Narayan, *Dislocating Cultures: Identities, Traditions, and Third-World Feminism*, Thinking Gender series (New York: Routledge, 1997), 63–68.

over the world, and colonization also succeeded in forever altering what it means to be British.

But Smith goes on to say: "There are still young white men who are angry about that: who will roll out at closing time into the poorly lit streets with a kitchen knife wrapped in a tight fist."[31] That is, Smith ties the phenomenon of Paki-bashing to a rejection of British identity as hopelessly bound up with the racial and ethnic identities of former colonial subjects. The second responsibility involves changing a false narrative of identity as ethnic purity to a narrative that more accurately reflects the reality that British identity now includes a multitude of different ethnic and racial identities and histories.

This new narrative of identity, however, must also incorporate the dynamics of exploitation that accompanied the colonial project in which Great Britain invaded and colonized other lands. When the British parliament decided that they could not accept this change in British identity, they turned away from the responsibilities that these historical relationships had wrought. The result was a deeper entrenchment of relationships of injustice. Justice as responsibility to relationships in this case would have included preferentially admitting migrants from former colonies because they were indeed fellows.

But that is not what happened, and it is not what is happening today. Justice requires seeing potential migrants from former colonies as fellows rather than strangers. This would be the first step toward right relationships with migrants and their descendants.

Guest Workers, Their Descendants, and Citizens

This third category of historical relationship mirrors in some ways the account of responsibilities to migrants from former colonies. We must retell the narratives of guest-worker programs in Western democracies in order to examine the ideological foundations of racism and ethnocentrism in those programs, including the living and working conditions of these guest workers. Like the citizens of former colonies, guest workers have changed the identity of their host countries. The guest-worker program changed Germany, for example, from a relatively homogeneous nation into the multicultural state it is today.[32] In the wake of reunification, guest workers at a violent anti-foreigner protest in Berlin carried signs that read, "Wir sind auch

31. Smith, *White Teeth*, 237.
32. Chin, *The Guest Worker Question in Postwar Germany*, 270–71.

das Volk" ("We are the people, too"). Like the British, Germans and citizens of other countries with guest-worker programs must retell the narrative of their own identity that incorporates the descendants of guest workers who have now legally become Germans.

While the migration systems initiated by guest-worker programs have in some cases ended, it is still possible to think about what these narratives of relationships and identity mean for right relationships today. I draw two conclusions. The guest-worker programs and relationships of the past can lead citizens to think more carefully about the policy decisions of the present. In the United States, guest-worker programs are occasionally floated as a policy solution to the problem of undocumented migration, despite the fact that the United States did have its own postwar guest-worker program, the *bracero* program, which had some of the same problems that the guest-worker programs of Western Europe did. Thus, if the false narratives of the past are not contested, history will repeat itself in more unjust policies.

Justice as responsibility to relationships would require that governments today learn from the narratives of the past. While I am suspicious about whether guest-worker programs can be built on just relationships at all, Michael Walzer writes that guest-worker programs can be just only if citizens see guest workers not as permanent outsiders but as potential new members.[33] In other words, not only must there be a path to citizenship written into the policy for guest workers who elect to stay in the host country; guest workers must be seen as full humans embedded in familial networks, rather than disconnected laborers. Thus, family reunification for guest workers should be a part of guest-worker policies.

Citizens, Their Corporations, and Migrants

The fourth category of historical relationships, foreign investment, is the category in which it is most difficult to make absolute statements concerning what just relationships would look like. In the case of the US relationship with Mexico, labor recruitment through both governmental and private initiatives brought Mexican guest workers to the United States. Foreign investment in export-oriented factories was layered on top of guest-worker programs and operated in tandem with them. The examination of the complicated relationship between Mexico and the United States indicates that

33. Walzer, *Spheres of Justice*, 62.

the relationships of responsibility between the two countries are vast and complex. The narratives about economic integration, foreign investment, and migration are just a few in a long and complex history.

Despite the fact that these narratives omit more than they reveal, they do give us grounds to contest the false narrative that Mexicans are an undifferentiated mass of poor people who are desperate to enter the United States. The specific relationship generated by private actors and corporations with specific cities and towns in Mexico have implications for the broader narrative of relationships between US and Mexican citizens, because investing in export-oriented factories is the result of broader economic policy decisions by the US and Mexican governments. These policy decisions have disproportionately benefited US citizens through the manufacture of cheap goods.[34]

Seeing export-oriented factories as the result of structural sin allows us to retell a narrative of the relationship between US citizens and Mexican migrants as one in which Mexican factory workers were reduced to the cost of their labor. Once they were deemed too expensive—in comparison to their counterparts in Central America and Southeast Asia—they were discarded. However, export-oriented factories are also the result of structural sin that inaugurated specific kinds of relationships between US consumers and Mexican factory workers. The neglect of US consumers' responsibility in these relationships led to the migration system, because, had US consumers seen the factory workers in their full humanity, the closing and relocation of those factories would not have gone unnoticed. But US consumers did not protest the closing of Mexico's factories, nor did they as a whole take notice of the working conditions and wages at those factories before they closed. As a result, when those factories did close, they created a migration system that increased Mexican migration to the United States just as US immigration and border-control policies grew harsher.

At this point, responsibility for relationships with undocumented migrants involves recognizing that their presence in the United States is the result of a migration system that has its roots in the actions of the US government and corporations. Extending full citizenship to undocumented Mexican migrants is not a matter of amnesty or forgiveness for their supposed transgressions; rather, it is a recognition of the history of the ongoing relationship between the two parties.

34. Obviously, economic integration has also benefited Mexico's economic elite; US citizens are not the only ones who have responsibilities to Mexico's factory workers. The owners of those factories might also have specific responsibilities.

Right Relationship and Structural Justice

In this examination of the four kinds of relationships that have initiated migration systems and the responsibilities that derive from them, I have referred to the fact that, in each case, extending full citizenship to these populations is a major part of fulfilling citizen responsibilities to them. Indeed, without full citizenship, migrants remain unable to fully participate in the society in which they live. Their status as resident aliens keeps them in a social position vis-à-vis citizens in which they can be easily exploited as cheap labor. With full citizenship, migrants can claim some of the social protections that are granted to citizens. However, citizenship for migrants is insufficient for the realization of justice as responsibility. While migrants who become citizens are technically members of the political community and thus should be bound by the same social contract that lays out the responsibilities that members have for each other, many of these new citizens and their children are still not accepted by members of the political communities as their equals. Many encounter discrimination, poverty, and lack of full access to adequate education. Full citizenship is thus necessary, but not sufficient, for right relationships with migrants and their descendants.

One way to account for the fact that citizen-migrants remain excluded from the full benefits and protections of the social contract is that the political and economic institutions of many liberal democracies remain unjust. They fail to regulate the inequalities, as John Rawls suggests, that they should. The children of migrants who lack social capital, education, and inherited wealth are thus hampered all their lives by the disadvantages suffered by their parents. While Rawls would say that institutions should be regulated so that inequalities do not compound over generations, justice as responsibility to relationships pays attention to the ground of our responsibilities to one another. The exclusion of the citizen-migrants and their descendants from certain benefits of the social contract, and their disproportionate share of the burdens, are the direct result of the refusal of citizens to accurately understand the relationship they have with migrants. In refusing to acknowledge their responsibilities, they have compounded the relationship of exploitation.

Therefore, while Rawls's ideal theory can describe how inequalities should be regulated, it cannot account for the history of false narratives and failed responsibilities. Reform of institutions cannot take place apart from the reform of the relationships between citizens of a nation-state and the descendants of its migrants. Ultimately, however, a changed relationship between citizens and their peers who are the descendants of migrants must result in a change in the social institutions to ensure a more just distribution of social benefits and burdens. Policies such as affirmative action, investing in schools where migrants cluster, and attending to "integration" must not be rooted in the desire to make the children of migrants more like citizens or to reduce crime rates and gang membership because they inconvenience or endanger citizens. Rather, they must be based on seeking a just relationship between migrants and citizens, one that remembers the contributions that migrants make to the host country.

Determining the responsibilities that emerge from relationships involves examining our accounts of those relationships and ensuring that they are accurate; meeting the responsibilities that emerge involves transforming relationships between migrants and citizens. This transformation involves structural changes such as granting citizenship to migrants and reforming certain domestic structures to ensure that migrants and their children are fully included. Of course, these policy proposals are nothing new. Christian ethicists and other political philosophers have been recommending justice for migrants for decades. My proposal differs, not on the basis of particular policy proposals, but on the grounds of citizens' responsibility toward migrants. Citizens' responsibilities toward migrants are grounded, not in an abstract cosmopolitanism, but in historical and concrete relationships that result in specific responsibilities toward migrants.

Justice, Solidarity, and the Rights of Migrants

If justice is responsibility to relationships, then how do we transform relationships of exploitation to relationships characterized by justice? How do we examine the veracity of our own narratives and replace them with better narratives? Justice as responsibility to relationships is impossible without solidarity: the work of transforming particular relationships of exploitation into relationships of justice. If justice is fulfilling responsibilities to relationships, solidarity is the work of transforming unjust relationships into just ones.

While a comprehensive account of solidarity is beyond the scope of this book, this brief account of solidarity pairs with justice as responsibility to relationships. My definition of solidarity is based in large part on Jon Sobrino's paradigmatic example of solidarity, drawn from the Salvadoran civil war, during which North American churches established relationships with Salvadoran churches. In Sobrino's analysis, these practices most closely mirror the parable of the Good Samaritan: "[These churches] have not taken a detour in order to avoid seeing the wounded victim on the road, but instead have come closer to examine the situation and help."[35] But Sobrino's account of solidarity has a key difference with the universalist interpretation of the Good Samaritan that I critically presented in chapter 1: it is based on the building and strengthening of particular relationships. These relationships are characterized by "co-responsibility," in which each party has responsibilities to the other. Solidarity is thus not simply the duty of benevolence, the duty to help someone in great need when the risk to oneself is low. Nor is it Rawls's duty of mutual aid, the temporary, short-term aid that liberal democracies must give to burdened societies only until they can become self-sufficient.[36] Rather, solidarity requires the establishment of lasting relationships, ones in which the parties are truly affected by each other's suffering. These relationships must be between unequals who "bear each other's burdens" as a part of their responsibility to one another.

Sobrino thus has an account of solidarity that depends on the cultivation of particular relationships. Though solidarity as a principle may be rooted in universal humanity, the practice of solidarity takes place between particular persons or groups. In Christopher Steck's words, "There is no generic relationship of solidarity, only concrete, particular instances."[37] Given the demands of solidarity as Sobrino describes them, and the limitations of our time, energy, and resources, it is unlikely that anyone would be able to extend solidarity to all the world's suffering. And this leaves us with a difficult set of questions that mirror the questions of the ethics of migration: How do we determine with whom we will build relationships of solidarity? With the most needy? The most proximate? What about those who are left out of the circles of proximity? A revision of Sobrino's account of solidarity can answer these questions.

Relationships bind people all over the world. Distant strangers may have no connection to us, but they may also be the strangers who slaughter our meat, sew our garments, or have recently lost jobs because a garment factory moved elsewhere. They may be people with whom we have connections, but these relationships are hidden by the same structures of sin that bind us to

35. Jon Sobrino, *The Principle of Mercy: Taking the Crucified People from the Cross* (Maryknoll, NY: Orbis, 1994), 144.

36. Sobrino, *Where Is God?* 18–23.

37. Steck, "Solidarity, Citizenship, and Globalization," 163.

these strangers. The further apart people are, the easier it is for their relationship to be characterized by exploitation. Solidarity, then, is the process of becoming aware of the historical and particular relationships we have with others—both near and far.

In a revised account of Sobrino's case study, the US churches did not establish relationships with Salvadoran churches out of nowhere. While the individual members of each local church may have been strangers to one another, US citizens were already in relationship with Salvadorans. The relationship between US citizens and Salvadorans was characterized by the quasi-colonial intervention of the US government into the affairs of the Salvadoran peoples, an intervention that furthered US ideological and economic interests at the expense of the poorest Salvadorans. The churches that reached out to Salvadoran churches were reaching out in defiance of the foreign policy of their government and changing the relationship between Salvadorans and Americans. In other words, they were not establishing relationships with strangers; they were turning relationships that had been formed by structures of sin into relationships characterized by the co-responsibility that Sobrino describes. The process of transforming these relationships is the work of solidarity. And this transformation cannot occur without a substantial investment of time and resources on behalf of both parties in the relationship.

Onora O'Neill argues that solidarity is an imperfect duty with no corollary universal right: in other words, everyone has a duty to solidarity, but no one has the right to the solidarity of another. I disagree with O'Neill. While there is no universal right to solidarity, there are special claims of solidarity, owed on the basis of particular unjust relationships. Given the number and extent of unjust relationships that structure our lives in a globalized world, deciding to whom we should extend solidarity is a complicated and fraught task that requires careful examination of our relationships and commitments. This is a matter not of universal principles but of particular judgment.

The US churches that entered into solidarity relationships with the Salvadoran churches made particular judgments about whom they would devote their time, energy, and resources to. Perhaps this judgment was based on feelings of responsibility based on US intervention in the Salvadoran civil war. Or perhaps it was based on the fact that, despite differences of nationality, ethnicity, and language, the US churches realized that they had duties of solidarity to Salvadoran churches based on a shared identity as Christians. Needless to say, solidarity in this case was not a matter of building a relationship out of nothing; it was about recognizing a concrete, historical relationship embedded in structural sin. And these churches resisted the structural sin by turning their relationships with the Salvadoran churches into relationships of solidarity.

If justice is responsibility to relationships that are institutionalized in both domestic and institutional structures, solidarity is the process and the practice that transform relationships of exploitation and domination into just relationships. Justice as responsibility to relationships is impossible to achieve without solidarity. And in the case of relationships between citizens and migrants, the changes to immigration and domestic policy required are also impossible without solidarity.

Justice as responsibility to relationships demands that some categories of immigrants are treated as fellow citizens; this requires changes in both immigration policy and domestic policy. However, changes in policy alone are insufficient for the full realization of justice because such changes cannot happen apart from the will of the political community. Viewing potential migrants as others to whom we may have responsibilities based on historical relationships rather than as helpless or opportunistic strangers requires citizens to change the central narratives about themselves and about potential migrants. This is not an easy—or likely—task. Solidarity, representing the practices by which citizens can recognize false narratives and transform relationships with migrants and potential migrants, is required for the full realization of justice because just institutions themselves require just relationships.

For Further Reading

For more comprehensive accounts of the theologies and philosophies of responsibility, see William Schweiker, *Responsibility and Christian Ethics* (Cambridge: Cambridge University Press, 1995); see also Albino Barrera, *Market Complicity and Christian Ethics* (Cambridge: Cambridge University Press, 2011).

Margaret Urban Walker's *Moral Understandings* (New York: Routledge, 1998) provides the foundations of my account of the relationship between narratives and responsibilities. This subtle and complex work is worth reading in full.

Iris Marion Young's posthumously published *Responsibility for Justice* (Oxford: Oxford University Press, 2011) provides ways of thinking about corporate rather than individual responsibility.

The Good Samaritan Revisited

In chapter 1, I highlighted the problems with using the Good Samaritan as a parable about the ethical imperative to care for strangers: the parable is about a chance encounter between strangers. The Samaritan does not appear to be weighing competing obligations, either between his family and this wounded Jew or among various strangers who need his help. The Good Samaritan seems to be a classic case study of "purely episodic dependence": moral responsibilities are clear because there is no narrative of relationship or competing responsibilities to contend with.[1] Relationships between migrants and citizens are not these kinds of episodic encounters: rather, they take place within thick historical contexts.

If we attempt to extend the moral lessons of episodic dependence to questions of global justice, including questions of justice toward migrants, the parable cannot tell us how to sort through competing obligations. It does not tell us which strangers have what kind of claims on us. However, read in its historical context, it is not a parable of purely episodic dependence; nor is the moral of the parable one about the praiseworthiness of benevolence toward strangers. In its historical context, the parable reveals the relationship among justice, relationships, and narratives.

New Testament and Jewish studies scholar Amy-Jill Levine points out that the Jews and Samaritans of the first century would not have regarded one another as strangers; instead, "they were all too familiar neighbors and all too hated enemies."[2] In other words, the encounter between the Samar-

---

1. Walker, *Moral Understandings*, 98.
2. Amy-Jill Levine, *Short Stories by Jesus: The Enigmatic Parables of a Controversial Rabbi* (New York: HarperOne, 2014), 74. Hereafter, page references to this work appear in parentheses within the text.

itan and the Jew takes place within the historical context of enmity. This enmity does not, in fact, emerge from radical differences; it emerges from similarities. The original Samaritans, like the Jews, were descended from the twelve tribes of Israel. Before Samaria was conquered by the Assyrians in the seventh century BCE, the Samaritans and Jews were neighbors in the Northern and Southern kingdoms of Israel. However, the relationship between Samaritans and Jews came to be marred over a long history of wrongs and failed responsibilities of one group toward the other. The Jews resented the Samaritans for not coming to their aid during the Jewish rebellion against the Greeks in 165 BCE; but the Samaritans came to have their own grievances against the Jews in 128 BCE, when the Jewish king destroyed the Samaritan temple (98). The parable of the Good Samaritan alludes to this enmity between Jews and Samaritans in order to cast the Samaritan—the enemy—as the one who helps someone in mortal peril.

Levine emphasizes that Jesus's Jewish audience almost certainly would not have heard this parable as a universal moral imperative to help a stranger in need, nor would they have identified with the Samaritan who ministers to the wounded stranger. In Jesus's context, the fact that the Samaritan turned out to be the one to offer compassion would have been disturbing, even shocking. Instead of taking from the story a universal moral imperative, Jesus's audience may have heard in it echoes of a story from 2 Chronicles, in which the Samaritan army loots a Judean city, captures thousands of women and children, and deports them to Samaria for slave labor (102–3). But that isn't the end of the story. Listening to Oded, a Hebrew prophet, denounce the Samaritan army, the leaders of Samaria have a change of heart: they clothe the captives, feed them, and anoint them. Then they take them to their kin in the Judean city of Jericho.

In the context of a relationship marked by a history of mutual antagonism, both 2 Chronicles and the parable of the Good Samaritan show how, regardless of their history of mutual antagonisms and grievances, people can establish different relationships—ones marked by care and concern for a specific "other." Levine concludes that the "cycle of violence can be broken" (103). Christian ethicists are correct to point to this parable as a paradigmatic example of solidarity for "others" who are suffering. However, separated from its historical context—the enmity between Jews and Samaritans—the parable reduces solidarity to an isolated act of charity. But in its context, the parable tells a different story: the Samaritan's actions are the very beginning of the possibility of a changed relationship between Jews and Samaritans. Recalling the narrative from 2 Chronicles for an audience who would have been fully aware of it, Jesus reminds them that "good Samaritan" is not an oxymoron. Whether the relationship between Jews and Samaritans can be transformed depends on the response of Jesus's listeners to the parable. Can they interrogate and then transform their own narrative about the Samaritans? Going forward, can they tell a new story?

The particular and specific historical relationship between the Samaritans and Jews turns the parable of the Good Samaritan from a parable about general benevolence to a parable about a particular relationship. Likewise, though the legal material concerning the *gēr* appears to be merely a set of rules, these rules draw heavily on the particular relationship between God and the Israelites, which sets the norms for the relationships between the Israelites and the *gērim* in their land. Justice, as we have seen, has a relational dimension that requires joining responsibilities to relationships; determining what these relationships are depends on having accurate narratives. These narratives are important when debating questions of justice toward fellow citizens, and they become even more important when there is no social contract underlying our relationships with others. Without some account of our responsibilities to one another, there can be no social contract.

At the same time, justice as responsibility to relationships does not dispense with universals altogether. It is crucial that the basic structure of any society distribute goods justly. There is a role for domestic institutions and for laws that aim at equality; likewise, international institutions are crucial for pointing to the distance between the ideal and the reality of where the world is today. Institutions also establish a legal minimum. For example, international refugee laws prohibit the repatriation of political refugees once they have left their countries.[3] Refugees must also be protected by positive rights that protect a dignified life. However insufficient these legal minimums are for specifying the allocation of responsibility for the rights of migrants, they are an important safeguard against the most egregious human-rights violations. However, neither just domestic institutions nor just international institutions can by themselves bring about justice. They can only help us avoid the most horrific kinds of injustices.

Justice as responsibility to relationships is sensitive to the particularities of relationships and histories. It admits the possibility of ambiguities and conflicts even in determining what our responsibilities are. We might not be able to meet all our responsibilities; we might not even be able to accurately

3. United Nations, "The 1951 Convention Relating to the Status of Refugees," http://www.unhcr.org/en-us/1951-refugee-convention.html.

determine what these responsibilities are. Rather than see this as a limitation of justice as responsibility, this admission of contingency and limitation resonates with the Augustinian tradition. In the words of Karen Lebacqz, "[Justice] is incomplete and fragile. Sometimes it will fail."[4] Perfect justice— which I define here as when we can individually and corporately meet all of our responsibilities to all of our relationships—will only come with the fullness of the heavenly city. By contrast, the earthly city is characterized as only a shadow of the perfect justice of the heavenly city. Meeting all of our responsibilities, or even knowing with certainty where we are meeting our responsibilities and where we are failing, might prove impossible. But the effort extended in discovering reality through relationships is the work of solidarity, and it is the only way to attain even the imperfect justice that is available in the earthly city.

I have argued that specific migrant populations in Germany, the United States, and the United Kingdom are owed specific goods, specifically the good of citizenship. I have also pointed to the ways in which citizenship is not sufficient to meet the conditions of justice: we also need structural justice in order for citizens to meet their responsibilities to specific migrants. But the reality of our relationality is substantially more complicated than these specific examinations might lead us to believe. In the United States, Germany, and the United Kingdom, and in countries all over the world, many different kinds of relationships lead to many different migration flows. The United States, for example, has migration flows initiated by foreign investment, by colonial and quasi-colonial foreign policies, and by guest-worker programs. How do these relationships with specific populations of migrants and the responsibilities that derive from them interact with one another? How do these responsibilities interact with responsibilities to distant others all over the globe?

Then there are political refugees, a category of migrant that I have largely left aside in this book. Some political refugees, like the Vietnamese refugees mentioned by Michael Walzer, were uprooted in part by actions of the host country, but this is not always the case. What responsibilities do host countries have to political refugees in cases where host countries may not share responsibility for having turned people into refugees? How do these responsibilities interact with responsibilities in which the relationship between citizens and migrants is more obvious?

Justice as responsibility to relationships cannot provide any unified

4. Lebacqz, *Justice in an Unjust World*, 147.

metric for sorting through competing responsibilities that derive from complicated historical relationships. Instead, justice as responsibility can shed light on these questions by providing a way to think through what our responsibilities might be. What is our history with these people? Where do they fit into our narratives? Do our narratives reflect the truth about our relationships? What foreign and economic policy decisions have affected this particular migration flow, and how? The answers to these questions are not obvious; nor will they be beyond debate or contestation. They are questions to be debated and wrestled with in the public sphere. If we are in part constituted by our relationships and our histories, wrestling with these questions is necessary not only for discovering our responsibilities but also for discovering our identities. They speak to the heart of who we are and who we want to be.

Bibliography

Abreu, Alexandre. "The New Economics of Labour Migration: Beware of Neoclassicals Bearing Gifts." *Forum for Social Economics* 41, no. 1 (2012): 46–67.

Adichie, Chimamanda Ngozi. "The Danger of a Single Story." TED: Ideas Worth Spreading, October 2009, https://www.ted.com/talks/chimamanda_adichie_the _danger_of_a_single_story/transcript?language=en.

Ahn, Ilsup. *Religious Ethics and Migration: Doing Justice to Undocumented Workers.* New York: Routledge, 2014.

Appiah, Kwame Anthony. "Cosmopolitan Patriots." In *For Love of Country?* edited by Martha Nussbaum and Joshua Cohen, 21–29. Boston: Beacon, 1996.

Arango, Joaquin. "Explaining Migration: A Critical View." *International Social Science Journal* 52, no. 3 (2000): 283–96.

Arendt, Hannah. *The Origins of Totalitarianism.* New York: Schocken Books, 2004.

Baggio, Fabio, and Agnes M. Brazal. *Faith on the Move: Toward a Theology of Migration in Asia.* Quezon City: Ateneo de Manila University Press, 2008.

Bakewell, Oliver. "Some Reflections on Structure and Agency in Migration Theory." *Journal of Ethnic and Migration Studies* 36, no. 10 (2010): 1689–1708.

Barbieri, William A. *Ethics of Citizenship: Immigration and Group Rights in Germany.* Durham, NC: Duke University Press, 1998.

Barrera, Albino. *Market Complicity and Christian Ethics.* Cambridge: Cambridge University Press, 2011.

Bartsch, Matthias, Andrea Brandt, and Daniel Steinvorth. "Turkish Immigration to Germany: A Sorry History of Self-Deception and Wasted Opportunities." *Spiegel Online*, September 7, 2010.

Bauder, Harald. *Labor Movement: How Migration Regulates Labor Markets.* Oxford: Oxford University Press, 2005.

Beitz, Charles R. *Political Theory and International Relations.* Princeton: Princeton University Press, 1979.

Birch, Bruce C. *Let Justice Roll Down: The Old Testament, Ethics, and Christian Life.* Louisville: Westminster John Knox, 1991.

Borjas, George J. *Friends or Strangers: The Impact of Immigrants on the U.S. Economy.* New York: Basic Books, 1990.

_____. *Heaven's Door: Immigration Policy and the American Economy.* Princeton: Princeton University Press, 1999.

Bosniak, Linda. "Human Rights, State Sovereignty, and the Protection of Undocumented Migrants under the International Migrant Workers Convention." *International Migration Review* 25, no. 4 (1991): 737–70.

Bosniak, Linda, and Aristide Zolberg. "State Sovereignty, Human Rights and the New UN Migrant Workers Convention." *Proceedings of the Annual Meeting, American Society of International Law* (1992): 634–41.

Bovani, Pietro. *Re-establishing Justice: Legal Terms, Concepts, and Procedures in the Hebrew Bible.* Translated by Michael J. Smith. Journal for the Study of the Old Testament Supplement Series 105. Sheffield, UK: JSOT Press, 1994.

Brazal, Agnes M., and María T. Dávila, eds. *Living with(out) Borders: Catholic Theological Ethics on the Migration of Peoples.* Maryknoll, NY: Orbis, 2016.

Brettell, Caroline B., and James F. Hollifield. "Introduction: Migration Theory." In *Migration Theory: Talking across Disciplines,* edited by Caroline B. Brettell and James F. Hollifield, 1–26. New York: Routledge, 2000.

Brueggemann, Walter. *The Land: Place as Gift, Promise, and Challenge in Biblical Faith.* 2nd ed. Minneapolis: Fortress, 2002.

Butt, Daniel. "Colonialism and Postcolonialism." In *The International Encyclopedia of Ethics,* edited by Hugh LaFollette, 892–98. Oxford: Wiley-Blackwell, 2013.

_____. *Rectifying International Injustice: Principles of Compensation and Restitution between Nations.* Oxford: Oxford University Press, 2009.

Campese, Gioacchino. "Beyond Ethnic and National Imagination." In *Religion and Social Justice for Immigrants,* edited by Pierrette Hondagneu-Sotelo, 175–90. New Brunswick: Rutgers University Press, 2007.

_____. "¿cuantos Más?: The Crucified Peoples at the U.S.-Mexico Border." In *A Promised Land, a Perilous Journey: Theological Perspectives on Migration,* edited by Daniel G. Groody and Gioacchino Campese, 271–98. Notre Dame, IN: University of Notre Dame Press, 2008.

Carens, Joseph H. "Aliens and Citizens: The Case for Open Borders." *The Review of Politics* 49, no. 2 (1987): 251–73.

_____. *The Ethics of Immigration.* New York: Oxford University Press, 2013.

Castles, Stephen. "Development and Migration—Migration and Development: What Comes First?" *Migration and Development: Future Directions for Research and Policy* 2 (2008). Social Science Research Council Migration and Development conference papers (pp. 10–32). New York: SSRC, February 28–March 1, 2008.

_____. "The Factors That Make and Unmake Migration Policy." In *Rethinking Migration: New Theoretical and Empirical Perspectives,* edited by Alejandro Portes and Josh DeWind, 31–63. New York: Berghahn Books, 2007.

_____. "Understanding Global Migration: A Social Transformational Perspective." *Journal of Ethnic and Migration Studies* 36, no. 10 (2010): 1565–86.

Castles, Stephen, and Mark J. Miller. *The Age of Migration: International Population Movements in the Modern World.* 4th rev. ed. New York: Guilford, 2009.

Chin, Rita C.-K. *The Guest Worker Question in Postwar Germany.* Cambridge: Cambridge University Press, 2007.

Christiansen, Drew. "Movement, Asylum, Borders: Christian Perspectives." *International Migration Review* (1996): 7–17.

_____. "*Pacem in Terris.*" In *Modern Catholic Social Teaching: Commentaries and Interpretations*, edited by Kenneth R. Himes et al. Washington, DC: Georgetown University Press, 2005.

Clark, Meghan J. *The Vision of Catholic Social Thought.* Minneapolis: Fortress, 2014.

Cohen, Matty. "Le 'ger' biblique et son statut socio-religieux." *Revue de l'histoire des religions* 207 (1990): 131–38.

Crüsemann, Frank. "'You Know the Heart of a Stranger' (Exodus 23:9): A Recollection of Torah in the Face of New Nationalism and Xenophobia." In *Migrants and Refugees*, edited by Dietmar Mieth and Lisa Sowle Cahill, 95–109. Maryknoll, NY: Orbis, 1993.

Cruz, Gemma Tulud. *An Intercultural Theology of Migration: Pilgrims in the Wilderness.* Boston: Brill, 2010.

_____. *Toward a Theology of Migration: Social Justice and Religious Experience.* New York: Palgrave Macmillan, 2014.

De Vaux, Roland. *Ancient Israel: Its Life and Institutions.* Translated by John McHugh. Grand Rapids: Eerdmans, 1997.

Donahue, John R. "The Bible and Catholic Social Teaching." In *Modern Catholic Social Teaching: Commentaries and Interpretations*, edited by Kenneth R. Himes et al., 9–40. Washington, DC: Georgetown University Press, 2004.

_____. "Biblical Perspectives on Justice." In *The Faith That Does Justice*, edited by John Haughey. New York: Paulist Press, 1977.

Estabrook, Barry. *Tomatoland: How Modern Industrial Agriculture Destroyed Our Most Alluring Fruit.* Kansas City, MO: Andrews McMeel Publishing, 2011.

Faist, Thomas. "Migrants as Transnational Development Agents: An Inquiry into the Newest Round of the Migration-Development Nexus." *Population, Place, and Space* 14 (2008): 21–42.

_____. *The Volume and Dynamics of International Migration and Transnational Social Spaces.* Oxford: Clarendon Press, 2000.

Faist, Thomas, Margit Fauser, and Peter Kivisto. *The Migration-Development Nexus: A Transnational Perspective.* New York: Palgrave Macmillan, 2011.

Farley, Margaret A. "Feminism and Universal Morality." In *Prospects for a Common Morality*, edited by Gene Outka and John P. Reeder, 170–90. Princeton: Princeton University Press, 1993.

_____. "A Feminist Version of Respect for Persons." *Journal of Feminist Studies in Religion* 9, nos. 1–2 (1993): 183–98.

_____. *Just Love: A Framework for Christian Sexual Ethics.* New York: Continuum International, 2006.

Ferraro, Vincent. "Dependency Theory: An Introduction." In *The Development Economics Reader*, edited by Giorgi Secondi, 58–64. New York: Routledge, 2008.

Finn, Daniel, ed. *Distant Markets, Distant Harms*. Oxford: Oxford University Press, 2014.

Francis, Pope. *Apostolic Exhortation Evangelii Gaudium of the Holy Father Francis to the Bishops, Clergy, Consecrated Persons and the Lay Faithful on the Proclamation of the Gospel in Today's World*. Vatican: Vatican Press, 2013. http://w2.vatican.va/content /francesco/en/apost_exhortations/documents/papa-francesco_esortazione-ap _20131124_evangelii-gaudium.html.

_____. *Encyclical Letter Laudato si' of the Holy Father Francis on Care for Our Common Home*. Vatican: Vatican Press, 2015. http://w2.vatican.va/content/francesco/en /encyclicals/documents/papa-francesco_20150524_enciclica-laudato-si.html.

_____. "Migrants and Refugees: Towards a Better World." Message of His Holiness Pope Francis for the World Day of Migrants and Refugees (2014). Vatican, August 5, 2013. http://w2.vatican.va/content/francesco/en/messages/migration/documents /papa-francesco_20130805_world-migrants-day.html.

Frey, Christopher. "The Impact of the Biblical Idea of Justice on Present Discussions of Social Justice." In *Justice and Righteousness: Biblical Themes and Their Influence*, edited by Henning Graf Reventlow and Yair Hoffman, 91–104. Sheffield, UK: Sheffield Academic Press, 1992.

Goldberg, Michael. *Jews and Christians, Getting Our Stories Straight: The Exodus and the Passion-Resurrection*. Philadelphia: Trinity Press International, 1991.

Gonzáles, Faus, and José Ignacio. "Sin." In *Mysterium Liberationis: Fundamental Concepts of Liberation Theology*, edited by Ignacio Ellacuría and Jon Sobrino, 532–42. Maryknoll, NY: Orbis, 1993.

Goodin, Robert. "What Is So Special about Our Fellow Countrymen?" In *Global Justice: Seminal Essays*, edited Thomas Pogge and Darrel Moellendorf, 255–84. St. Paul: Paragon House, 2008.

Gosselin, Abigail. "Global Poverty and Responsibility: Identifying the Duty-Bearers of Human Rights." *Human Rights Review* 8, no. 1 (2006): 35–52.

Groody, Daniel G. *Border of Death, Valley of Life: An Immigrant Journey of Heart and Spirit*. Lanham: Rowman and Littlefield, 2002.

Groody, Daniel G., and Gioacchino Campese, eds. *A Promised Land, a Perilous Journey: Theological Perspectives on Migration*. Notre Dame, IN: University of Notre Dame Press, 2008.

Gutiérrez, Gustavo. "Poverty, Migration, and the Option for the Poor." In *A Promised Land, a Perilous Journey: Theological Perspectives on Migration*, edited by Daniel G. Groody and Gioacchino Campese, 76–86. Notre Dame, IN: University of Notre Dame Press, 2008.

Hahamovitch, Cindy. *No Man's Land: Jamaican Guestworkers in America and the Global History of Deportable Labor*. Princeton: Princeton University Press, 2011.

Hays, Richard B. *The Moral Vision of the New Testament: Community, Cross, New Creation; A Contemporary Introduction to New Testament Ethics*. San Francisco: HarperSanFrancisco, 1996.

Heimbach-Steins, Marianne. "The Ambivalence of Borders and the Challenge of an Ethics of Liminality." In *Living with(out) Borders: Catholic Theological Ethics on the Migration of Peoples*, edited by Agnes M. Brazal and María Teresa Dávila, 236–46. Maryknoll, NY: Orbis, 2016.

Hendel, Ronald. *Remembering Abraham: Culture, Memory, and History in the Hebrew Bible*. New York: Oxford University Press, 2005.

Heyer, Kristin E. *Kinship across Borders: A Christian Ethic of Immigration*. Washington, DC: Georgetown University Press, 2012.

_____. "Social Sin and Immigration: Good Fences Make Bad Neighbors." *Theological Studies* 71 (2010): 410–36.

_____. "Strangers in Our Midst: Day Laborers and U.S. Immigration Reform." *Political Theology* 9, no. 4 (2008): 425–53.

Himes, Kenneth R. "Human Failing: The Meanings and Metaphors of Sin." In *Moral Theology: New Directions and Fundamental Issues*, edited by James Keating. New York: Paulist Press, 2004.

Himes, Kenneth R., et al., eds. *Modern Catholic Social Teaching: Commentaries and Interpretations*. Washington, DC: Georgetown University Press, 2005.

Hollenbach, David. *Claims in Conflict: Retrieving and Renewing the Catholic Human Rights Tradition*. Woodstock Studies 4. New York: Paulist Press, 1979.

Hollenbach, David, ed. *Driven from Home: Protecting the Rights of Forced Migrants*. Washington, DC: Georgetown University Press, 2010.

_____, ed. "Internally Displaced People, Sovereignty, and the Responsibility to Protect." In *Refugee Rights: Ethics, Advocacy, and Africa*, edited by David Hollenbach, 177–93. Washington, DC: Georgetown University Press, 2008.

_____, ed. *Refugee Rights: Ethics, Advocacy, and Africa*. Washington, DC: Georgetown University Press, 2008.

Hollifield, James Frank. "The Politics of International Migration: How Can We 'Bring the State Back In'?" In *Migration Theory: Talking across Disciplines*, edited by Caroline B. Brettel and James F. Hollifield, 137–85. New York: Routledge, 2000.

House of Bishops of the Episcopal Church. "The Nation and the Common Good: Reflections on Immigration Reform." The Episcopal Church, September 21, 2010, http://archive.episcopalchurch.org/documents/HOB_theological_resource_on _immigration.pdf.

_____. "A Pastoral Letter from the House of Bishops." The Episcopal Church, September 21, 2010, http://www.episcopalchurch.org/notice/house-bishops-issues -pastoral-letter-along-theological-resource-%C2%93-nation-and-common-good -refl.

Huntington, Samuel P. *Who Are We? The Challenges to America's National Identity*. New York: Simon and Schuster, 2004.

Jaggar, Alison M. *Feminist Politics and Human Nature*. Philosophy and Society 1. Totowa, NJ: Rowman and Allanheld, 1983.

John XXIII. *Pacem in terris*. In *Catholic Social Thought: The Documentary Heritage*, edited by David J. O'Brien and Thomas A. Shannon, 131–62. Maryknoll, NY: Orbis, 1992.

John Paul II. "Ecclesia in America." January 22, 1999. http://w2.vatican.va/content
/john-paul-ii/en/apost_exhortations/documents/hf_jp-ii_exh_22011999_ecclesia
-in-america_en.html.

———. *Laborem exercens*. Encyclical letter. Castel Gandolfo, Italy, September 14, 1981.
http://w2.vatican.va/content/john-paul-ii/en/encyclicals/documents/hf_jp-ii
_enc_14091981_laborem-exercens.html.

———. "Letter to Archbishop John-Louis Tauran on the Occasion of the Twenty-First-
Century Slavery—The Human Rights Dimension of Trafficking in Human Beings" (2002). The Holy See, http://w2.vatican.va/content/john-paul-ii/en/letters
/2002/documents/hf_jp-ii_let_20020515_tauran.html.

———. *Sollicitudo Rei Socialis*. In *Catholic Social Thought: The Documentary Heritage*,
edited by David J. O'Brien and Thomas A. Shannon. Maryknoll, NY: Orbis, 1992.

———. "Undocumented Migrants." Message of Pope John Paul II for World Migration
Day, 1996. Vatican, July 25, 1995. http://w2.vatican.va/content/john-paul-ii/en
/messages/migration/documents/hf_jp-ii_mes_25071995_undocumented_mi
grants.html.

Johnson, B. "Mishpat." In *Theological Dictionary of the Old Testament*, edited by G. Johannes Botterweck and Helmer Ringgren, vol. 9. Grand Rapids: Eerdmans, 1974.

———. "Sedeq." In *Theological Dictionary of the Old Testament*, ed. G. Johannes Botterweck and Helmer Ringgren, vol. 12. Grand Rapids: Eerdmans, 1974.

Joppke, Christian. *Immigration and the Nation-State: The United States, Germany, and
Great Britain*. Oxford: Oxford University Press, 1999.

Kanstroom, Dan. *Deportation Nation: Outsiders in American History*. Cambridge, MA:
Harvard University Press, 2007.

Kellerman, D. "Gēr, Gur." In *Theological Dictionary of the Old Testament*, edited by
G. Johannes Botterweck and Helmer Ringgren, vol. 2. Grand Rapids: Eerdmans,
1974.

Kerwin, Donald. "The Natural Rights of Migrants and Newcomers: A Challenge to U.S.
Law and Policy." In *A Promised Land, a Perilous Journey: Theological Perspectives
on Migration*, edited by Daniel G. Groody and Gioacchino Campese, 192–209.
Notre Dame, IN: University of Notre Dame Press, 2008.

———. "Rights, the Common Good, and Sovereignty." In *And You Welcomed Me: Migration and Catholic Social Teaching*, edited by Donald Kerwin and Jill Marie Gerschutz, 93–121. Lanham, MD: Lexington Books, 2009.

Kerwin, Donald, and Jill Marie Gerschutz, eds. *And You Welcomed Me: Migration and
Catholic Social Teaching*. Lanham, MD: Lexington Books, 2009.

King, Russell, and Ronald Skeldon. "Mind the Gap: Integrating Approaches to Internal
and International Migration." *Journal of Ethnic and Migration Studies* 36, no. 10
(2010): 1619–46.

Köhler, Ludwig, Walter Baumgartner, M. E. J. Richardson, and Johann Jakob Stamm.
The Hebrew and Aramaic Lexicon of the Old Testament. Study ed. Boston: Brill,
2001.

Kritz, Mary M, and Hania Zlotnik. "Global Interactions: Migration Systems, Processes,
and Policies." In *International Migration Systems: A Global Approach*, edited by

Mary M. Kritz, Lin Lean Lim, and Hania Zlotnik, 1–34. Oxford: Clarendon Press, Oxford University Press, 1992.

Kritz, Mary M., Lin Lean Lim, and Hania Zlotnik. *International Migration Systems: A Global Approach.* International Studies in Demography series. Oxford: Clarendon Press, Oxford University Press, 1992.

LaCugna, Catherine. *God for Us: The Trinity and Christian Life.* New York: HarperOne, 1991.

Laegaard, Sune. "David Miller on Immigration Policy and Nationality." *Journal of Applied Philosophy* 24, no. 3 (2007): 283–98.

Lebacqz, Karen. *Justice in an Unjust World: Foundations for a Christian Approach to Justice.* Minneapolis: Augsburg, 1987.

———. *Six Theories of Justice: Perspectives from Philosophical and Theological Ethics.* Minneapolis: Augsburg, 1986.

Lee, Everett S. "A Theory of Migration." *Demography* 3, no. 1 (1966): 47–57.

Levine, Amy-Jill. *Short Stories by Jesus: The Enigmatic Parables of a Controversial Rabbi.* New York: Harper One, 2014.

Lim, Lin Lean. "International Labor Movements: A Perspective on Economic Exchanges and Flows." In *International Migration Systems: A Global Approach*, edited by Mary M. Kritz, Lin Lean Lim, and Hania Zlotnik, 133–49. Oxford: Clarendon Press, Oxford University Press, 1992.

Lu, Catherine. "Colonialism as Structural Injustice: Historical Responsibility and Contemporary Redress." *Journal of Political Philosophy* 19, no. 3 (2011): 261–81.

MacIntyre, Alasdair C. *After Virtue: A Study in Moral Theory.* 2nd ed. Notre Dame, IN: University of Notre Dame Press, 1984.

Maritain, Jacques. *Man and the State.* Washington, DC: Catholic University of America Press, 1998.

Martínez, Oscar J. "Migration and the Border, 1965–1985." In *Beyond La Frontera: The History of Mexico-U.S. Migration*, edited by Mark Overmyer-Velázquez, 103–21. New York: Oxford University Press, 2011.

Massey, Douglas S. "Why Does Immigration Occur? A Theoretical Synthesis." In *The Handbook of International Migration: The American Experience*, edited by Charles Hirschman, Philip Kasinitz, and Josh DeWind, 34–52. New York: Russell Sage Foundation, 1999.

Massey, Douglas S., Jorge Durand, and Nolan J. Malone. *Beyond Smoke and Mirrors: Mexican Immigration in an Era of Economic Integration.* New York: Russell Sage Foundation, 2002.

Massey, Douglas S., Joaquin Arango, Graeme Hugo, Adela Pellegrino, and J. Edward Taylor. *Worlds in Motion: Understanding International Migration at the End of the Millennium.* Oxford: Oxford University Press, 2005.

Mieth, Dietmar, and Lisa Sowle Cahill. *Migrants and Refugees.* Maryknoll, NY: Orbis, 1993.

Miller, David. "Immigrants, Nations, and Citizenship." *Journal of Political Philosophy* 16, no. 4 (2008): 371–90.

_____. "Irregular Migrants: An Alternative Perspective." *Ethics and International Affairs* 22, no. 2 (2008): 163–86.

_____. *National Responsibility and Global Justice.* Oxford: Oxford University Press, 2007.

Narayan, Uma. *Dislocating Cultures: Identities, Traditions, and Third-World Feminism.* Thinking Gender series. New York: Routledge, 1997.

Nazario, Sonia. *Enrique's Journey: The Story of a Boy's Dangerous Odyssey to Reunite with His Mother.* New York: Random House, 2014.

Nussbaum, Martha C. *Creating Capabilities: The Human Development Approach.* Cambridge, MA: Belknap Press, Harvard University Press, 2011.

_____. *Frontiers of Justice: Disability, Nationality, Species Membership.* Cambridge, MA: Belknap Press, Harvard University Press, 2006.

_____. *Women and Human Development: The Capabilities Approach.* The John Robert Seeley lectures. Cambridge: Cambridge University Press, 2000.

O'Brien, David J., and Thomas A. Shannon. *Catholic Social Thought: The Documentary Heritage.* Maryknoll, NY: Orbis, 1992.

Oezcan, Veysel. "Germany: Immigration in Transition." Migration Information Source, July 1, 2004, http://www.migrationinformation.org/feature/display.cfm?ID=235.

Ogletree, Thomas W. *Hospitality to the Stranger: Dimensions of Moral Understanding.* Louisville: Westminster John Knox, 2003.

O'Neill, Onora. *Bounds of Justice.* Cambridge: Cambridge University Press, 2000.

_____. "Christian Hospitality and Solidarity with the Stranger." In *And You Welcomed Me: Migration and Catholic Social Teaching,* edited by Donald Kerwin and Jill Marie Gerschutz, 149–55. Lanham, MD: Lexington Books, 2009.

_____. *Towards Justice and Virtue: A Constructive Account of Practical Reasoning.* Cambridge: Cambridge University Press, 1996.

O'Neill, William. "'No Longer Strangers' (Ephesians 2:19): The Ethics of Migration." *Word and World* 29, no. 3 (2009): 227–33.

O'Neill, William, and William C. Spohn. "Rights of Passage: The Ethics of Immigration and Refugee Policy." *Theological Studies* 59 (1998): 84–106.

Overmyer-Velázquez, Mark. *Beyond La Frontera: The History of Mexico-U.S. Migration.* New York: Oxford University Press, 2011.

Papademetriou, Demetrios G. "The Shifting Expectations of Free Trade and Migration." In *NAFTA's Promise and Reality: Lessons from Mexico for the Hemisphere* (2004): 39–60. Carnegie Endowment for International Peace, 2004, http://carnegie endowment.org/files/nafta1.pdf.

Pedersen, Johannes, and Fru Aslaug (Mikkelsen) Møller. *Israel, Its Life and Culture.* Vol. 1. London: Oxford University Press, 1926.

Pius XII. *Exsul Familia Nazarethana.* Papal Encyclicals Online, August 1, 1952, http://www.papalencyclicals.net/Pius12/p12exsul.htm.

Pogge, Thomas. "An Egalitarian Law of Peoples." *Philosophy and Public Affairs* 23, no. 3 (1994): 195–224.

_____. *World Poverty and Human Rights: Cosmopolitan Responsibilities and Reforms.* Cambridge, MA: Polity, 2002.

Pogge, Thomas, and Darrel Moellendorf, eds., *Global Justice: Seminal Essays*. St. Paul, MN: Paragon House, 2008.

Pohl, Christine D. "Hospitality from the Edge: The Significance of Marginality in the Practice of Welcome." *Annual for the Society of Christian Ethics* 15, no. 1 (2001): 126.

Polaski, Sandra. "Jobs, Wages, and Household Income." *NAFTA's Promise and Reality: Lessons from Mexico for the Hemisphere* (2004): 11–38. Carnegie Endowment for International Peace, 2004, http://carnegieendowment.org/files/nafta1.pdf.

Porter, Jean. "The Virtue of Justice (IIa IIae, Qq. 58–122)." In *The Ethics of Aquinas*, edited by Stephen J. Pope, 273–86. Washington, DC: Georgetown University Press, 2002.

Portes, Alejandro. "Immigration Theory for a New Century: Some Problems and Opportunities." *International Migration Review* 31, no. 4 (1997): 799–825.

_____. "Migration and Social Change: Some Conceptual Reflections." *Journal of Ethnic and Migration Studies* 36, no. 10 (2010): 1537–63.

Portes, Alejandro, and József Böröcz. "Contemporary Immigration: Theoretical Perspectives on Its Determinants and Modes of Incorporation." *International Migration Review* 23, no. 3 (1989): 606–30.

Portes, Alejandro, and Josh DeWind. *Rethinking Migration: New Theoretical and Empirical Perspectives*. New York: Berghahn Books, 2007.

Rajendra, Tisha M. "Justice, Not Benevolence: Catholic Social Thought, Migration Theory, and the Rights of Migrants." *Political Theology* 15, no. 3 (2014): 290–306.

_____. "The Rational Agent or the Relational Agent: Moving from Freedom to Justice in Migration Systems Ethics." *Ethical Theory and Moral Practice* 18 (2015): 355–69.

Ramírez Kidd, José E. *Alterity and Identity in Israel: The [Gēr] in the Old Testament*. New York: Walter de Gruyter, 1999.

Rawls, John. *Justice as Fairness: A Restatement*. Edited by Erin Kelly. Cambridge, MA: Harvard University Press, 2001.

_____. *The Law of Peoples*. Cambridge, MA: Harvard University Press, 1999.

_____. *Political Liberalism*. Columbia Classics in Philosophy series. Expanded ed. New York: Columbia University Press, 2005.

_____. *A Theory of Justice*. Cambridge, MA: Belknap Press, Harvard University Press, 1971.

Regan, Margaret. *The Death of Josseline: Immigration Stories from the Arizona-Mexico Borderlands*. Boston: Beacon, 2010.

Reichman, Daniel. "Honduras: The Perils of Remittance Dependence and Clandestine Migration." Migration Information Source, April 11, 2013, http://www.migrationpolicy.org/article/honduras-perils-remittance-dependence-and-clandestine-migration/.

Ross, Susan A. *Anthropology: Seeking Light and Beauty*. Collegeville, MN: Liturgical Press, 2012.

Ruiz, Jean-Pierre. *Readings from the Edges: The Bible and People on the Move*. Maryknoll, NY: Orbis, 2011.

Sassen, Saskia. *Guests and Aliens*. New York: New Press, 1999.

_____. *Losing Control? Sovereignty in an Age of Globalization*. New York: Columbia University Press, 1996.

_____. *The Mobility of Labor and Capital: A Study in International Investment and Labor Flow*. Cambridge: Cambridge University Press, 1988.

_____. *Territory, Authority, Rights: From Medieval to Global Assemblages*. Princeton: Princeton University Press, 2006.

Schain, Martin. *The Politics of Immigration in France, Britain, and the United States: A Comparative Study*. New York: Palgrave Macmillan, 2008.

Scheffler, Samuel. *Boundaries and Allegiances: Problems of Justice and Responsibility in Liberal Thought*. Oxford: Oxford University Press, 2001.

Schiller, Nina Glick. "A Global Perspective on Migration and Development." In *Migration, Development, and Transnationalization: A Critical Stance*, edited by Nina Glick Schiller and Thomas Faist, 22–62. New York: Berghahn Books, 2010.

Schiller, Nina Glick, and Thomas Faist. *Migration, Development, and Transnationalization: A Critical Stance*. New York: Berghahn Books, 2010.

Schiller, Nina Glick, and Thomas Faist. "Introduction: Migration, Development, and Transformation." In *Migration, Development, and Transnationalization: A Critical Stance*, edited by Nina Glick Schiller and Thomas Faist, 1–21. New York: Berghahn Books, 2010.

Schweiker, William. *Responsibility and Christian Ethics*. New Studies in Christian Ethics series. Cambridge: Cambridge University Press, 1995.

_____. "Responsibility and Moral Realities." *Studies in Christian Ethics* 22, no. 4 (2009): 472–95.

Second Vatican Council. "Gaudium et Spes." In *Catholic Social Thought: The Documentary Heritage*, edited by David O'Brien and Thomas A. Shannon, 164–237. Maryknoll, NY: Orbis, 1992.

Sen, Amartya. *Development as Freedom*. New York: Anchor Books, 1999.

_____. "Rational Fools: A Critique of the Behavioral Foundations of Economic Theory." *Philosophy and Public Affairs* 6, no. 4 (1977): 317–44.

Senior, Donald. "'Beloved Aliens and Exiles': New Testament Perspectives on Migration." In *A Promised Land, a Perilous Journey: Theological Perspectives on Migration*, edited by Daniel Groody and Gioacchino Campese, 20–34. Notre Dame, IN: University of Notre Dame Press, 2008.

Skeldon, Ronald. *Migration and Development: A Global Perspective*. London: Addison-Wesley Longman Higher Education, 1997.

Smith, Zadie. *White Teeth*. New York: Random House, 2000.

Sobrino, Jon. "Central Position of the Reign of God in Latin American Liberation Theology." In *Mysterium Liberationis: Fundamental Concepts of Liberation Theology*, edited by Ignacio Ellacuría and Jon Sobrino, 350–88. Maryknoll, NY: Orbis, 1993.

_____. "Five Hundred Years: Structural Sin and Structural Grace." In *The Principle of Mercy: Taking the Crucified People from the Cross*, edited by Jon Sobrino, 69–82. Maryknoll, NY: Orbis, 1994.

_____. *The Principle of Mercy: Taking the Crucified People from the Cross*. Maryknoll, NY: Orbis, 1994.

_____. *Where Is God? Earthquake, Terrorism, Barbarity, and Hope.* Maryknoll, NY: Orbis, 2004.

Spina, Frank. "Israelites as *Gerim.*" In *The Word Shall Go Forth: Essays in Honor of David Noel Freedman,* edited by Carol L. Meyers and M. O'Connor. Winona Lake, IN: Eisenbrauns, 1992.

Stark, Oded, and J. Edward Taylor. "Migration Incentives, Migration Types: The Role of Relative Deprivation." *The Economic Journal* 101, no. 408 (1991): 1163–78.

_____. "Relative Deprivation and International Migration." *Demography* 26, no. 1 (1989): 1–14.

_____. "Relative Deprivation and Migration: Theory, Evidence, Policy Implications." In *Determinants of Emigration from Mexico, Central America, and the Caribbean,* edited by Sergio Diaz-Briquets and Sidney Weintraub, 121–44. Boulder, CO: Westview, 1991.

Steck, Christopher. "Solidarity, Citizenship, and Globalization: Developing a New Framework for Theological Reflections on U.S.-Mexico Immigration." *Journal of Peace and Justice Studies* 14, no. 2 (2004): 153–78.

Traina, Cristina L. H. "Facing Forward." In *Distant Markets, Distant Harms: Economic Complicity and Christian Ethics,* edited by Daniel K. Finn, 173–201. Oxford: Oxford University Press, 2014.

United Nations. "Declaration on the Granting of Independence to Colonial Countries and Peoples," December 14, 1960, http://www.un.org/ga/search/view_doc .asp?symbol=A/RES/1514(XV).

_____. "The 1951 Convention Relating to the Status of Refugees," http://www.unhcr .org/en-us/1951-refugee-convention.html.

_____. "The Universal Declaration of Human Rights," December 10, 1948, http://www .un.org/en/documents/udhr/index.shtml.

United States Conference of Catholic Bishops, and Conferencia del Episcopado Mexicano. "Strangers No Longer: Together on the Journey of Hope," January 22, 2003, http://www.usccb.org/issues-and-action/human-life-and-dignity/immigration /strangers-no-longer-together-on-the-journey-of-hope.cfm.

Van Hear, Nicholas. "Theories of Migration and Social Change." *Journal of Ethnic and Migration Studies* 36, no. 10 (2010): 1531–36.

von Rad, Gerhard. *Old Testament Theology.* Translated by D. M. G. Stalker. Vol. 1. New York: Harper, 1962.

Walker, Margaret Urban. *Moral Understandings: A Feminist Study in Ethics.* New York: Routledge, 1998.

Walzer, Michael. *Exodus and Revolution.* New York: Basic Books, 1985.

_____. *Spheres of Justice: A Defense of Pluralism and Equality.* New York: Basic Books, 1983.

_____. *What It Means to Be an American.* New York: Marsilio, 1992.

Weinfeld, Moshe. *Deuteronomy and the Deuteronomic School.* Winona Lake, IN: Eisenbrauns, 1992.

_____. *Social Justice in Ancient Israel and in the Ancient Near East.* Minneapolis: Fortress; Jerusalem: Magnes, 1995.

Wilbanks, Dana W. *Re-creating America: The Ethics of U.S. Immigration and Refugee Policy in a Christian Perspective.* Nashville: Abingdon, 1996.

Young, Iris Marion. *Justice and the Politics of Difference.* Princeton: Princeton University Press, 1990.

_____. *Responsibility for Justice.* Oxford: Oxford University Press, 2011.

Ypi, Lea. "Justice in Migration: A Closed Borders Utopia?" *Journal of Political Philosophy* 16, no. 4 (2008): 391–418.

Yuengert, Andrew, and Gloria L. Zúñiga. *Inhabiting the Land: The Case for the Right to Migrate.* Grand Rapids: Acton Institute, 2003.

Zolberg, Aristide R. "The Next Waves: Migration Theory for a Changing World." *International Migration Review* 23, no. 3 (1989): 403–30.

Index of Authors

Index of Subjects

Agency-dominant theories of migration, 33, 35–41, 47, 48; feminist ethics and autonomy-in-relation, 33, 39–40, 49, 74, 119; liberalism and the assumption of primacy of rationality, 39–40; neoclassical migration theory, 9, 35–41, 50, 51–52, 125–26; new economics of migration, 35–36, 38–41, 50; and public discussions of immigration and undocumented migrants, 40–41; and Rawls's philosophical migration ethics, 40

Aquinas, Thomas, 117

Austria, 1

Capabilities approach to global justice (Nussbaum), 9, 87–92, 118, 120

Castro, Mario Alapizco, 11–12, 16–18, 21–22, 26–29, 86

Catholic social teaching, 5, 20–23, 90, 117

Christian ethics of migration, 8–9, 11–30; cosmopolitanism in, 14–15; foundational principles and limitations, 8–9, 11–30; and human-rights discourse, 8–9, 12, 13–23; and interdisciplinary field of migration theory, 32–33, 45–46, 52; and justice in the Hebrew Bible, 111–12; Kew Gardens Principle, 28–30; linking the right of migration to duty, 18–19, 20–23; and parable of the Good Samaritan, 24–25, 29, 139, 142–44; and preferential option for the poor, 8–9, 23–28; and universal human-rights discourse, 8–9, 12, 13–23. *See also* Justice as responsibility to relationships

Citizenship for migrants, 65–66, 137, 145

Colonial migration systems, 7, 63–67, 133–34; differences from foreign-investment-driven migration, 70; effect on the colonizing nation, 66–67; France, 46, 64, 65–66; racial ideologies, 65–66; responsibilities of citizens of former colonial powers to colonial migrants and their descendants, 133–34; as structural injustice, 64; United Kingdom and its former colonial subjects, 7, 55, 63–67, 70, 73, 133–34; unjust policies and domination, 63–64, 66, 133–34

Communitarians, 4, 73–74, 91–92

Contractarian approaches to global justice (Rawls), 9, 77–82, 91, 117–18, 123, 137; and a bounded society/liberal democratic society, 76, 77–79–82; communal self-determination, 79; the difference principle, 77–79; the duty of assistance, 79–80; the equal opportunity principle, 77–78; the equality liberty principle, 77–78; and justice as a virtue of social

Index of Scripture References